Daily Quotes from Famous Women of The Planet

1258 Inspirational and Motivational Quotes for Positive Thinking, Self-Esteem, Success, Money, Wealth, Health, Love, Happiness and More

Darleen Mitchell

TABLE OF CONTENTS

INTRODUCTION

This book is a treasure chest, a secret box of feminine wisdom, wit, causticity, and generosity. Here are collected quotes and aphorisms of the most famous, outstanding, bright, brave and strong women of our world, whose talent and belief in themselves have changed it for better. There is a lot that we can learn from these women...

Open it on any page, select the line and find out what awaits you next, take a sneak peek in your future. This book will be a source of inspiration for all who feel the desire to realize themselves and move towards their goals.

ANGELINA JOLIE

Angelina Jolie (born June 4, 1975) is an American actress, filmmaker, and humanitarian. She has received an Academy Award, two Screen Actors Guild Awards, and three Golden Globe Awards, and has been cited as Hollywood's highest-paid actress. She is also known for her humanitarian and activist work in Africa and the Middle East. She continues to be a role model and inspires millions to be confident & powerful people who change the world.

* * *

I've realized that being happy is a choice. You never want to rub anybody the wrong way or not be fun to be around, but you have to be happy.

* * *

If I make a fool of myself, who cares? I'm not frightened by anyone perception of me.

* * *

People have two sides, a good side, and a bad side, a past, a future. We must embrace both in someone we love.

* * *

We have a responsibility to be aware of others.

* * *

If you ask people what they've always wanted to do,
most people haven't done it. That breaks my heart.

* * *

Different is good. When someone tells you that you
are different, smile and hold your head up and be proud.

* * *

People always slow down for a train wreck. It's like
junk food. If you don't feel good about yourself, you
want to read crap about other people, like gossip in high
school. You don't understand why it's there, but
somehow it makes a lot of people feel better. 8. If I
didn't have my films as an outlet for all the different
sides of me, I would probably be locked up.

* * *

I'm very happy and very excited when my adrenalin is
going.

* * *

Nothing would mean anything if I didn't live a life of
use to others.

* * *

Be brave, be bold, be free.

* * *

We have a choice about how we take what happens to us in our life and whether or not we allow it to turn is. We can become consumed by hate and darkness, or we can regain our humanity somehow, or come to terms with things and learn something about ourselves.

* * *

It is not where you start in life that counts the most; it is how you choose to face it.

* * *

You'd think, 'what if I make a mistake today, I'll regret it.' I don't believe in regret, I feel everything leads us to where we are, and we have just to jump forward, mean well, commit and see what happens.

* * *

Every day we choose who we are by how we define ourselves.

* * *

Life comes with many challenges. The ones that should not scare us are the ones we can take on and take control of. 17. I am a strong believer that without justice, there is no peace. No lasting peace anyway.

* * *

If I think more about death than some other people, it is probably because I love life more than they do I've never lived my life in the opinion of others. I believe I'm a good person. I believe I'm a good mom. But that's for my kids to decide, not for the world.

* * *

I never felt settled or calm. You can't commit to live when you feel that.

* * *

I've been reckless, but I'm not a rebel without a cause.

* * *

Wherever I am, I always find myself looking out the window wishing I was somewhere else.

* * *

Make bold choices and make mistakes. It's all those things that add up to the person you become.

* * *

I'm not somebody that thinks about destiny and fate,
but I don't walk away from it when something unfolds.

* * *

People say that you're going the wrong way when it's
simply a way of your own.
Figure out who you are separate from your family,
and the man or woman you're in a relationship with.
Find who you are in this world and what you need to feel
good alone. I think that's the most important thing in
life. Find a sense of self because, with that, you can do
anything else.

* * *

Love – is when you wish all the best to the people you
love when you put their interests and well-being above
their own. Always.

* * *

It's better to have nobody than to have someone who
is half there or doesn't want to be there.

* * *

I have so much in my life. I want to be of value to the
world.

* * *

If you don't get out of the box you've been raised in,
you won't understand how much bigger the world is.

* * *

If every choice you make comes from an honest place,
you're solid, and nothing anybody can say about you can
rock you or change your opinion.

* * *

We come to love not by finding the perfect person, but
by learning to see an imperfect person perfectly.

* * *

I do believe in the old saying, 'what doesn't kill you
makes you stronger.' Out experiences, good and bad,
make us who we are. By overcoming difficulties, we
gain strength and maturity.

* * *

The truth is I love being alive. And I love feeling free.
So if I can't have those things, then I feel like a caged
animal, and I'd rather not be in a cage. I'd rather be
dead. And it's really simple. And I think it's not that
uncommon.

* * *

I like someone who is a little crazy but coming from a good place. I think scars are sexy because it means you made a mistake that led to a mess.

* * *

Our diversity is our strength. What a dull and pointless life it would be if everyone was the same.

* * *

There's something about death that is comforting. The thought that you could die tomorrow frees you to appreciate your life now.

* * *

I try to lead by example, being conscious of others and being responsible.

* * *

When I get logical, and I don't trust my instincts – that's when I get in trouble.

* * *

I'm happy being myself, which I've never been to before. I always hid in other people, or tried to find myself through the characters, or live out their lives, but I didn't have those things in mine.

* * *

Without pain, there would be no suffering; without suffering we would never learn from our mistakes. To make it right, pain and suffering is the key to all windows; without it, there is no way of life. 42. It's hard to be clear about who you are when you are carrying around a bunch of baggage from the past. I've learned to let go and more quickly into the next place.

AMELIA EARHART

Amelia Mary Earhart (born July 24, 1897; disappeared July 2, 1937) was an American aviation pioneer and author. Earhart was the first female aviator to fly solo across the Atlantic Ocean. She received the United States Distinguished Flying Cross for this accomplishment. She set many other records, wrote best-selling books about her flying experiences and was instrumental in the formation of The Ninety-Nines, an organization for female pilots. In 1935, Earhart became a visiting faculty member at Purdue University as an advisor to aeronautical engineering and a career counselor to women students. She was also a member of the National Woman's Party and an early supporter of the Equal Rights Amendment.

During an attempt to make a circumnavigational flight of the globe in 1937, Earhart and navigator Fred Noonan disappeared over the central Pacific Ocean near Howland Island. Fascination with her life, career, and disappearance continues to this day.

* * *

Please know that I am aware of the hazards. I want to do it because I want to do it. Women must try to do things as men have tried. When they fail, their failure must be but a challenge to others.

* * *

Courage is the price that life exacts for granting peace. The soul that knows it not, knows no release from little things, knows not the livid loneliness of fear.

* * *

The most difficult thing is the decision to act; the rest is merely tenacity. The fears are paper tigers. You can do anything you decide to do. You can act to change and control your life, and the procedure, the process is its reward.

* * *

No kind of action ever stops with itself. One kind of action leads to another. A good example is followed.

* * *

Women must pay for everything. They do get more glory than men for comparable feats, But they also get more notoriety when they crash.

* * *

Women, like men, should try to do the impossible. And when they fail, their failure should be a challenge to others.

* * *

Worry retards reaction and makes clear-cut decisions impossible.

* * *

The more one does and sees and feels, the more one can do, and the more genuine may be one's appreciation of fundamental things like home, and love, and understanding companionship.

* * *

Never interrupt someone doing something you said couldn't be done.

* * *

Adventure is worthwhile in itself.

* * *

A single act of kindness throws out roots in all directions, and the roots spring up and make new trees. The greatest work that kindness does to others is that it makes them kind themselves.

* * *

Anticipation, I suppose, sometimes exceeds realization.

* * *

In my life, I had come to realize that when things were going very well, indeed it was just the time to anticipate trouble. And, conversely, I learned from pleasant experience that at the most despairing crisis, when all looked sour beyond words, some delightful break was apt to lurk just around the corner.

* * *

I want to do something useful in the world.

* * *

Preparation, I have often said, is rightly two-thirds of any venture.

* * *

Being alone is scary, but not as scary as feeling alone in a relationship.

* * *

Better do a good deed near at home than go far away to burn incense.

* * *

Experiment! Meet new people. That's better than any college education.

* * *

After midnight the moon set and I was alone with the stars. I have often said that the lure of flying is the lure of beauty, and I need no other flight to convince me that the reason flyers fly, whether they know it or not, is the aesthetic appeal of flying.

* * *

Flying may not be all plain sailing, but the fun of it is worth the price.

* * *

ANNA ELEANOR ROOSEVELT

Anna Eleanor Roosevelt (October 11, 1884 – November 7, 1962) was an American political figure, diplomat and activist. She served as the First Lady of the United States from March 1933 to April 1945 during her husband President Franklin D. Roosevelt's four terms in office, making her the longest serving First Lady of the United States. Roosevelt served as United States Delegate to the United Nations General Assembly from 1945 to 1952. President Harry S. Truman later called her the "First Lady of the World" in tribute to her human rights achievements.

Roosevelt was a member of the prominent American Roosevelt and Livingston families and a niece of President Theodore Roosevelt. She had an unhappy childhood, having suffered the deaths of both parents and one of her brothers at a young age. At 15, she attended Allenwood Academy in London and was deeply influenced by its headmistress Marie Souvestre. Returning to the U.S., she married her fifth cousin once removed, Franklin Delano Roosevelt, in 1905. The Roosevelts' marriage was complicated from the beginning by Franklin's controlling mother, Sara, and after Eleanor discovered her husband's affair with Lucy Mercer in 1918, she resolved to seek fulfillment in public life of her own. She persuaded Franklin to stay in politics after he was stricken with a paralytic illness in 1921, which cost him the normal use of his legs and began giving speeches and appearing at campaign events in his place. Following Franklin's election as Governor of New York in 1928, *and throughout the remainder of Franklin's public career in government, Roosevelt regularly made public appearances on his behalf, and as First Lady, while her husband served as President, she significantly reshaped and redefined the role of First Lady.*

Though widely respected in her later years, Roosevelt was a controversial First Lady at the time for her outspokenness, particularly her stance on racial issues. She was the first presidential spouse to hold regular press conferences, write a daily newspaper column, write a monthly magazine column, host a weekly radio show, and speak at a national party convention. On a few occasions, she publicly disagreed with her husband's policies. She launched an experimental community at Arthurdale, West Virginia, for the families of unemployed miners, later widely regarded as a failure. She advocated for expanded roles for women in the workplace, the civil rights of African Americans and Asian Americans, and the rights of World War II refugees.

Following her husband's death in 1945, Roosevelt remained active in politics for the remaining 17 years of her life. She pressed the United States to join and support the United Nations and became its first delegate. She served as the first chair of the UN Commission on Human Rights and oversaw the drafting of the Universal Declaration of Human Rights. Later she chaired the John F. Kennedy administration's Presidential Commission on the Status of Women. By the time of her death, Roosevelt was regarded as "one of the most esteemed women in the world"; she was called "the object of almost universal respect" in her New York Times obituary. In 1999, she was ranked ninth in the top ten of Gallup's List of Most Widely

Admired People of the 20th Century.

* * *

Do what you feel in your heart to be right – for you'll be criticized anyway. You'll be damned if you do, and damned if you don't.

* * *

The future belongs to those who believe in the beauty of their dreams.

* * *

The purpose of life is to live it, to taste experience to the utmost, to reach out eagerly and without fear for newer and richer experience.

* * *

Do one thing every day that scares you.

* * *

You must do the things you think you cannot do.

* * *

A stumbling block to the pessimist is a stepping-stone to the optimist.

* * *

It is better to light a candle than curse the darkness.

* * *

You can often change your circumstances by changing your attitude.

* * *

Many people will walk in and out of your life, but only true friends will leave footprints in your heart.

* * *

Do one thing every day that scares you.

* * *

In the long run, we shape our lives, and we shape ourselves. The process never ends until we die. And the choices we make are ultimately our own responsibility.

* * *

Justice cannot be for one side alone but must be for both.

* * *

It takes courage to love, but pain through love is the purifying fire which those who love generously know.

* * *

If life were predictable, it would cease to be life, and be without flavor.

* * *

We are afraid to care too much, for fear that the other person does not care at all.

* * *

The only things one can admire at length are those one admires without knowing why.

* * *

The giving of love is an education in itself.

* * *

The battle for the individual rights of women is one of long standing, and none of us should countenance anything which undermines it.

* * *

Perhaps nature is our best assurance of immortality.

* * *

Sometimes I wonder if we shall ever grow up in our politics and say definite things which mean something, or whether we shall always go on using generalities to which everyone can subscribe, and which mean very little.

* * *

Happiness is not a goal... it's a by-product of a life well lived.

* * *

You gain strength, courage, and confidence by every experience in which you really stop to look fear in the face. You are able to say to yourself, 'I have lived through this horror. I can take the next thing that comes along.' You must do the thing you think you cannot do.

* * *

A woman is like a tea bag – you can't tell how strong she is until you put her in hot water.

* * *

To handle yourself, use your head; to handle others, use your heart.

* * *

Too often the great decisions are originated and given form in bodies made up wholly of men, or so completely dominated by them that whatever of special value women have to offer is shunted aside without expression.

* * *

Only a man's character is the real criterion of worth.

* * *

You wouldn't worry so much about what others think of you if you realized how seldom they do.

* * *

My experience has been that work is almost the best way to pull oneself out of the depths.

* * *

It isn't enough to talk about peace. One must believe in it. And it isn't enough to believe in it. One must work at it.

* * *

I think, at a child's birth if a mother could ask a fairy godmother to endow it with the most useful gift, that gift should be curiosity.

* * *

When will our consciences grow so tender that we will act to prevent human misery rather than avenge it?

* * *

Have convictions. Be friendly. Stick to your beliefs as they stick to theirs. Work as hard as they do.

* * *

Every time you meet a situation you think at the time it is an impossibility, and you go through the tortures of the damned, once you have met it and lived through it, you find that forever after you are freer than you were before.

* * *

I think that somehow, we learn who we really are and then live with that decision.

* * *

Beautiful young people are accidents of nature, but beautiful old people are works of art.

* * *

I once had a rose named after me, and I was very flattered. But I was not pleased to read the description in the catalog: no good in a bed, but fine up against a wall.

* * *

No one can make you feel inferior without your consent.

* * *

Do the things that interest you and do them with all your heart. Don't be concerned about whether people are watching you or criticizing you.

* * *

A little simplification would be the first step toward rational living, I think.

* * *

What you don't do can be a destructive force.

* * *

People grow through experience if they meet life honestly and courageously. This is how the character is built.

* * *

You gain strength, courage, and confidence by every experience in which you really stop to look fear in the face. You are able to say to yourself, 'I lived through this horror. I can take the next thing that comes along.

* * *

What one has to do usually can be done.

* * *

I think I lived those years very impersonally. It was almost as though I had erected someone outside myself who was the president's wife. I was lost somewhere deep down inside myself. That is the way I felt and worked until I left the White House.

* * *

Probably the happiest period in life most frequently is in middle age, when the eager passions of youth are cooled, and the infirmities of age not yet begun; as we see that the shadows, which are at morning and evening so large, almost entirely disappear at midday.

* * *

You can't move so fast that you try to change the mores faster than people can accept it. That doesn't mean you do nothing, but it means that you do the things that need to be done according to priority.

* * *

Courage is exhilarating.

* * *

With the new day comes new strength and new thoughts.

* * *

I'm so glad I never feel important, it does complicate life!

* * *

It is not fair to ask of others what you are not willing to do yourself.

* * *

In all our contacts it is probably the sense of being really needed and wanted which gives us the greatest satisfaction and creates the most lasting bond.

* * *

If someone betrays you once, it's their fault; if they betray you twice, it's your fault.

* * *

We do not have to become heroes overnight. Just a step at a time, meeting each thing that comes up, seeing it as not as dreadful as it appears, discovering that we have the strength to stare it down.

* * *

What could we accomplish if we knew we could not fail?

* * *

Probably the happiest period in life most frequently is in middle age, when the eager passions of youth are cooled, and the infirmities of age not yet begun; as we see that the shadows, which are at morning and evening so large, almost entirely disappear at midday.

* * *

You can never really live anyone else's life, not even your child's. The influence you exert is through your own life, and what you've become yourself.

* * *

Autobiographies are only useful as the lives you read about and analyze may suggest to you something that you may find useful in your own journey through life.

* * *

In the long run, we shape our lives, and we shape ourselves. The process never ends until we die. And the choices we make are ultimately our own responsibility.

* * *

Pit race against race, religion against religion, prejudice against prejudice. Divide and conquer! We must not let that happen here.

* * *

I can not believe that war is the best solution. No one won the last war, and no one will win the next war.

* * *

I do not think that I am a natural born mother... If I ever wanted to mother anyone, it was my father.

* * *

Old age has deformities enough of its own. It should never add to them the deformity of vice.

* * *

Never allow a person to tell you know who doesn't have the power to say yes.

* * *

One's philosophy is not best expressed in words; it is expressed in the choices one makes... and the choices we make are ultimately our responsibility.

* * *

As for accomplishments, I just did what I had to do as things came along.

* * *

I have never felt that anything really mattered but knowing that you stood for the things in which you believed and had done the very best you could.

* * *

You have to accept whatever comes and the only important thing is that you meet it with courage and with the best that you have to give.

* * *

The only advantage of not being too good a housekeeper is that your guests are so pleased to feel how very much better they are.

* * *

A mature person is one who does not think only in absolutes, who is able to be objective even when deeply stirred emotionally, who has learned that there is both good and bad in all people and in all things, and who walks humbly and deals charitably with the circumstances of life, knowing that in this world no one is all-knowing, and therefore all of us need both love and charity.

* * *

Great minds discuss ideas; average minds discuss events; small minds discuss people.

* * *

The reason that fiction is more interesting than any other form of literature, to those who really like to study people, is that in fiction the author can really tell the truth without humiliating himself.

* * *

Happiness is not a goal; it is a by-product.

* * *

Never mistake knowledge for wisdom. One helps you make a living; the other helps you make a life.

* * *

Ambition is pitiless. Any merit that it cannot use it finds despicable.

* * *

Since you get more joy out of giving joy to others, you should put a good deal of thought into the happiness that you are able to give.

* * *

Today is the oldest you've ever been, and the youngest you'll ever be again.

* * *

I used to tell my husband that, if he could make me 'understand' something, it would be clear to all the other people in the country.

* * *

Hate and force cannot be in just a part of the world without having an effect on the rest of it.

* * *

Understanding is a two-way street.

* * *

Freedom makes a huge requirement of every human being. With freedom comes responsibility. For the person who is unwilling to grow up, the person who does not want to carry his own weight, this is a frightening prospect.

*　*　*

One thing life has taught me: if you are interested, you never have to look for new interests. They come to you. When you are genuinely interested in one thing, it will always lead to something else.

*　*　*

Do not stop thinking of life as an adventure. You have no security unless you can live bravely, excitingly, imaginatively; unless you can choose a challenge instead of competence.

*　*　*

I have spent many years of my life in opposition, and I rather like the role.

*　*　*

Anyone who thinks must think of the next war as they would of suicide.

*　*　*

The mother of a family should look upon her housekeeping and the planning of meals as a scientific occupation.

* * *

I believe that anyone can conquer fear by doing the things he fears to do, provided he keeps doing them until he gets a record of successful experience behind him.

* * *

Life was meant to be lived, and curiosity must be kept alive. One must never, for whatever reason, turn his back on life.

* * *

When life is too easy for us, we must beware, or we may not be ready to meet the blows which sooner or later come to everyone, rich or poor.

* * *

Remember always that you have not only the right to be an individual; you have an obligation to be one. You cannot make any useful contribution in life unless you do this.

* * *

Never be bored, and you will never be boring.

* * *

I am who I am today because of the choices I made yesterday.

* * *

We have to face the fact that either all of us are going to die together or we are going to learn to live together, and if we are to live together, we have to talk.

* * *

Will people ever be wise enough to refuse to follow bad leaders or to take away the freedom of other people?

* * *

If you can develop this ability to see what you look at, to understand its meaning, to readjust your knowledge to this new information, you can continue to learn and to grow as long as you live and you'll have a wonderful time doing it.

* * *

Be confident, not certain.

* * *

He who learns but does not think is lost. He who thinks but does not learn is in great danger.

* * *

It takes as much energy to wish as it does to plan.

* * *

Life must be lived, and curiosity kept alive. One must never, for whatever reason, turn his back on life.

* * *

When you cease to make a contribution,
you begin to die.

* * *

It is not more vacation we need – it is more vocation.

* * *

Life is what you make it. Always has been,
always will be.

CHER

Cherilyn Sarkisian (born; May 20, 1946) is an American singer and actress. Commonly referred to by the media as the Goddess of Pop, she has been described as embodying female autonomy in a male-dominated industry. She is known for her distinctive contralto singing voice and for having worked in numerous areas of entertainment, as well as adopting a variety of styles and appearances during her six-decade-long career. Cher gained popularity in 1965 as one-half of the folk-rock husband-wife duo Sonny & Cher after their song "I Got You Babe" reached number one on the American and British charts. By the end of 1967, they had sold 40 million records worldwide and had become, according to Time magazine, rock's "it" couple. She began her solo career simultaneously, releasing in 1966 her first million-seller song, "Bang Bang (My Baby Shot Me Down)." She became a television personality in the 1970s with her shows The Sonny & Cher Comedy Hour, watched by over 30 million viewers weekly during its three-year run, and Cher. She emerged as a fashion trendsetter by wearing elaborate outfits on her television shows. Cher has won a Grammy Award, an Emmy Award, an Academy Award, three Golden Globe Awards, a Cannes Film Festival Award, a special CFDA Fashion Award, and a Kennedy Center Honors prize, among several other honors. She has sold 100 million records worldwide to date, becoming one of the best-selling music artists in history. She is the only artist to date to have a number-one single on a Billboard chart in six consecutive decades, from the 1960s to the 2010s. Outside of her music and acting, she is *noted for her political views, philanthropic endeavors, and social activism, including LGBT rights and HIV/AIDS prevention.*

* * *

The trouble with some women is that they get all excited about nothing – and then marry him.

* * *

A girl can wait for the right man to come along – but in the meantime that still doesn't mean she can't have a wonderful time with all the wrong ones.

* * *

Don't take your toys inside just because it's raining.

* * *

If grass can grow through cement, love can find you at every time in your life.

* * *

Men aren't necessities. They're luxuries.

* * *

God made a woman beautiful and foolish; beautiful, that man might love her; and foolish, that she might love him.

* * *

Anyone who's a great kisser I'm always interested in.
I haven't a clue why I've lasted so long. There's no
reason. There are many people more talented than me. I
think it's luck.

* * *

I only answer to two people, myself and God.

* * *

It's not necessary, to be a complete person, that I have
a man. It's not the end-all, be-all of my life.

* * *

In this business, you have to be tough, and if someone
pushes me far, I can certainly be impossible. I've always
said, if you're nice, they walk over you, and if you stand
up for yourself, they call you a bitch.

* * *

Women have to harness their power – it's true. It's just
learning not to take the first no. And if you can't go
straight ahead, you go around the corner.

* * *

I've always taken risks and never worried about what the world might think of me.

* * *

I can trust my friends. These people force me to examine myself, encourage me to grow.

* * *

Nothing lifts me out of a bad mood better than a hard workout on my treadmill. It never fails. To us, exercise is nothing short of a miracle.

* * *

I'm scared to death of being poor. It's like a fat girl who loses 500 pounds but is always fat inside. I grew up poor and will always feel poor inside.
It's my pet paranoia.

* * *

I'm a perfectionist, my own boss. If someone isn't pulling their weight, I let them know. I'm a nice person, but you can't say yes to everyone.

* * *

I don't read magazines; I don't like disposable culture.

* * *

I don't know what keeps me down to earth, but it sure isn't ironing. I send mine out.

* * *

Some years I'm the coolest thing that ever happened, and then the next year everyone's so over me, and I'm just so past my sell date.

* * *

If you are going to wait for someone to encourage you to do something, you just better give up.

* * *

Going hungry never bothered me – it had no clothes.

* * *

For better or worse, I never plan my life. I focus on today. I love spontaneity. That is what has put me in some strange and wonderful places in my life.

* * *

Hate crimes are the scariest thing in the world because these people really believe what they're doing is right.

* * *

I think that the longer I look good, the better gay men feel.

* * *

I won't be able to do what I'm doing forever. There aren't that many scripts floating around for fifty-year-old chicks.

* * *

If you really want something you can figure out how to make it happen.

* * *

I feel like a bumper car. If I hit a wall, I'm backing up and going in another direction. And I've hit plenty of fucking walls in my career. But I'm not stopping. I think maybe that's my best quality: I just don't stop.

* * *

Yes, it's a man's world, but that's all right because they're making a total mess of it. We're chipping away at their control, taking the parts we want. Some women think it's a difficult task, but it's not.

* * *

Husbands are like fires – they go out when they're left unattended.

* * *

Until you're ready to look foolish, you'll never have the possibility of being great. Don't need a man, but I'm happier with one. I like to have someone I can touch and squeeze and kiss. But I don't fold up and die if I don't have a man around.

* * *

Women are the real architects of society.

* * *

Some guy said to me, don't you think you're too old to sing rock n' roll? I said You'd better check with Mick Jagger.

* * *

Men should be like Kleenex – soft, strong and disposable.

* * *

I don't like Bush. I don't trust him. I don't like his record. He's stupid. He's lazy.

* * *

I'm not a role model, nor have I ever tried to be a role model. The only thing about me as a role model is I've managed to stay here and be working and survive. For 40 years. In this business, it takes time to be really good – and by that time, you're obsolete.

* * *

The truth is that in my job becoming old and becoming extinct are the same thing.

* * *

There are lots of things I'd like to be, and nice just doesn't seem good enough.

* * *

If you're black in this country if you're a woman in this country if you are any minority in this country at all, what could possess you to vote Republican?

* * *

Honesty makes me feel powerful in a difficult world.

* * *

Living your life, the way you want to live it is the most important thing so if you have to pay small prices along the way. It's not important. – Life is about enjoying yourself and having a good time.

COCO CHANEL

Gabrielle Bonheur "Coco" Chanel (19 August 1883 – 10 January 1971) was a French fashion designer and a businesswoman. She was the founder and namesake of the Chanel brand. Chanel was credited in the post-World War I era with liberating women from the constraints of the "corseted silhouette" and popularizing a sporty, casual chic as the feminine standard of style. A prolific fashion creator, Chanel extended her influence beyond couture clothing, realizing her design aesthetic in jewelry, handbags, and fragrance. Her signature scent, Chanel No. 5, has become an iconic product. She is the only fashion designer listed on TIME magazine's list of the 100 most influential people of the 20th century. Chanel designed her famed interlocked-CC monogram, meaning Coco Chanel, using it since the 1920s.

* * *

Some people think luxury is the opposite of poverty. It is not. It is the opposite of vulgarity.

* * *

The most courageous act is still to think for yourself. Aloud.

* * *

There is no time for cut-and-dried monotony. There is time for work. And time for love. That leaves no other time.

* * *

My life didn't please me, so I created my life.

* * *

I don't care what you think about me. I don't think about you at all.

* * *

Luxury must be comfortable. Otherwise, it is not luxury.

* * *

Simplicity is the keynote of all true elegance.

* * *

Don't spend time beating on a wall, hoping to transform it into a door.

* * *

Success is often achieved by those who don't know that failure is inevitable.

* * *

The most courageous act is still to think for yourself.
Aloud.

* * *

Dress shabbily, and they remember the dress; dress
impeccably, and they remember the woman.

* * *

Fashion fades, only style remains the same.

* * *

To be irreplaceable, one must always be different.

* * *

A girl should be two things: classy and fabulous.

* * *

A woman who doesn't wear perfume has no future.

* * *

The most courageous act is still to think for yourself.
Aloud.

* * *

If you were born without wings, do nothing to prevent them from growing.

* * *

Fashion is not something that exists in dresses only. Fashion is in the sky, in the street, fashion has to do with ideas, the way we live, what is happening.

* * *

I don't do fashion. I AM fashion.

* * *

As long as you know men are like children, you know everything!

* * *

Hard times arouse an instinctive desire for authenticity.

* * *

Dress like you are going to meet your worst enemy today.

* * *

It's probably not just by chance that I'm alone. It would be very hard for a man to live with me unless he's strong. And if he's stronger than I, I'm the one who can't live with him. ... I'm neither smart nor stupid, but I don't think I'm a run-of-the-mill person. I've been in business without being a businesswoman, I've loved without being a woman made only for love. The two men I've loved, I think, will remember me, on earth or in heaven, because men always remember a woman who caused them concern and uneasiness. I've done my best, regarding people and life, without precepts, but with a taste for justice.

CONNIE PODESTA

Connie Podesta (born 1975) Expert on High Performance, Leadership, Managing Change, Sales, and Communications.

Connie Podesta is a game-changing, idea-generating ball of fire whose rare blend of humor, substance, style, and personality have made her one of the most memorable, in-demand speakers in the world today.

* * *

I want to tell you something, women: Men aren't afraid of death, disease, torture or war. Do you know what wakes a man up in the middle of the night? In a cold sweat, the very thought that tomorrow, the very thought that tomorrow you will have him involved in a discussion about the relationship.

* * *

Standing out positively isn't something you do some of the time. It's something you strive for all the time. Your social media should reflect that.

* * *

Difficult people are great actors. Every difficult person in your life – will you see them for what they are? Don't take it personally. It isn't about you. They treat their spouse this way... Difficult people have an act. And they either use their whining crying to make you feel guilty, so that you'll give in, or they use anger to make you afraid so that you will give in. Difficult people want one thing – they want their own way.

* * *

Powerful motivational speaking is so much more than smart words and a polished delivery; it is that ability to reach inside the audience and touch their minds, hearts, and souls so they will truly want to experience outstanding results in every area of their life – both work and home.

* * *

Healthy relationships are based on one thing – healthy communication, otherwise known as assertive, or to get right to the point – adult communication.

* * *

The number 1 reason why someone has an affair in marriage is not about sex. It's because they no longer felt good about themselves in the presence of their spouse. The number 1 reason why an employee quits their job is not about money; it's because they no longer felt good about themselves in the presence of their management team. Ladies and gentleman, we make choices based on how we feel about ourselves.

* * *

I am choosing to be more creative, more passionate, more productive, and more confident than ever before. Why? Because I have no other choice if I want to succeed. And, believe me, success is not an option for me; and hopefully, not for you either. Ready to tackle the world? Then start with a change and a choice. Change any attitudes and behaviors that may get in your way and sabotage your success. And choose to forge ahead with spirit, determination and a lot of love along the way.

* * *

Sometimes in our attempt to give children what we did not have, we forget to give our children what we did have.

* * *

The game of life is basically about getting our needs met.

* * *

Fairness isn't a given. Watch out for the warning signs and choose to surround yourself with people who play fair, work fair and live life with integrity.

* * *

Too often people let the past be about regrets and the future be about worry. Neither emotion is going to get your needs met, make you a better person, increase your ability to love and be loved, mend a heart, or solve a problem... at this moment.

* * *

The way we communicate is changing at lightning speed. If you want to out-think, out-perform the competition and be valued, you've got to change with it.

* * *

Women, shame on you! Don't you ever ask a man in your life again about your weight? You have a scale – get on it!

* * *

Difficult people have been trained and taught to act the way they do since they were children. In fact, they have been rewarded for their negative behavior throughout their entire lives. Difficult behavior worked for them as children, and more importantly, it continues to work for them as adults.

* * *

Change is what makes life exciting, daring, different, inspired. Stop fighting it. Embrace it!

* * *

There's enough negative in the world to go around. My goals mirror those of most top leaders. People need real positive change today. They need to see possibilities where others see obstacles. They need to feel empowered rather than powerless. And they need real-world solutions to help them achieve these things. That's what I can bring to the table.

* * *

We are not attracted to people because of their strengths; we are attracted to people because of our weaknesses. Which is why it is so important that you understand yourself.

* * *

If you don't understand people – customers, colleagues, leaders, owners, family, friends and yourself, there is NO WAY you can ever experience success – at any level

* * *

You are not your past. And your future? Will take care of itself – if you choose to live.

* * *

Indifferent and apathetic people are just as dangerous to your life as negative people.
Apathy is contagious!

* * *

Men are so much better getting their needs met... If a guy has a need, he goes after it. Doesn't worry about it, doesn't feel guilty about it, he just moves on, gets it met, goes to the next step... Women, we have come so far. Professionally. We have broken every glass ceiling there is to break. We are CEOs of major companies; women are coaches of major sports teams, we are prime ministers of countries. Yet, do you know that the average woman today is no better at getting her personal needs met than she was a hundred years ago?

* * *

Communication is one of the most vital tools we can harness in terms of building better companies and better relationships. How you present yourself in person and now through social media platforms speaks volumes to your character, integrity and frankly, they are deciding factors for people to determine whether they want to do business with you.

* * *

Happiness is understanding that abundance is yours for the taking.

* * *

Memories can either make you or break you. They can drag you down, destroy your confidence, wear out your spirit and keep you living in what was and not what is. Or they can be the foundation for unbelievable learning, new experiences, and a purposeful, happy life built on what you are capable of achieving at this very moment in time. Don't live in the past – learn from it.

* * *

Procrastination? Career-killer. Joy-spoiler. Relationship-ender. Don't wait for tomorrow to be happier and more successful.

HARRIET TUBMAN

Harriet Tubman (born 1822–1913) was an American abolitionist and political activist. Born into slavery, Tubman escaped and subsequently made some thirteen missions to rescue approximately seventy enslaved people, family, and friends, using the network of antislavery activists and safe houses known as the Underground Railroad. She later helped abolitionist John Brown recruit men for his raid on Harpers Ferry. During the Civil War, she served as an armed scout and spy for the United States Army. In her later years, Tubman was an activist in the struggle for women's suffrage.

Born a slave in Dorchester County, Maryland, Tubman was beaten and whipped by her various masters as a child. Early in life, she suffered a traumatic head wound when an irate slave owner threw a heavy metal weight intending to hit another slave but hit her instead. The injury caused dizziness, pain, and spells of hypersomnia, which occurred throughout her life. She was a devout Christian and experienced strange visions and vivid dreams, which she ascribed to premonitions from God.

In 1849, Tubman escaped to Philadelphia, then immediately returned to Maryland to rescue her family. Slowly, one group at a time, she brought relatives with her out of the state, and eventually guided dozens of other slaves to freedom. Traveling by night and in extreme secrecy, Tubman (or "Moses," as she was called) "never lost a passenger." After the Fugitive Slave Act of 1850 was passed, she helped guide fugitives farther north into British North America and helped newly freed slaves find work. Tubman met the abolitionist John Brown in 1858, and helped him plan and recruit supporters for the raid on Harpers Ferry.

When the Civil War began, Tubman worked for the Union Army, first as a cook and nurse, and then as an armed scout and spy. The first woman to lead an armed expedition in the war, she guided the raid at Combahee Ferry, which liberated more than 700 slaves. After the war, she retired to the family home on property she had purchased in 1859 in Auburn, New York, where she cared for her aging parents. She was active in the women's suffrage movement until illness overtook her and she had to be admitted to a home for elderly African Americans that she had helped to establish years earlier. After she died in 1913, she became an icon of the courage and freedom of African-Americans.

In 2016, it was decided to place the portrait of Harriet Tubman on a $ 20 bill in place of President Andrew Jackson, a former slave trader and a hardliner against the native Indian population. The idea came from the initiative group Women on twenty-dollar bills (Women On 20s), which set its goal in 2020 to mark the centenary of providing women with voting rights as a portrait of a woman on a dollar bill. Most of the participants in the online survey voted for Tubman, which allowed her to bypass 14 other candidates, including Eleanor Roosevelt, Rosa Parks and the first Cherokee woman Wilma Mankiller. It is noteworthy that women were depicted on the banknote of twenty dollars: the goddess of Freedom in 1863 and Pocahontas in 1865.

✳ ✳ ✳

Every great dream begins with a dreamer. Always remember, you have within you the strength, the patience, and the passion to reach for the stars to change the world

* * *

I freed a thousand slaves I could have freed a thousand more if only they knew they were slaves.

* * *

I had reasoned this out in my mind; there was one of two things I had a right to, liberty or death; if I could not have one, I would have the other.

* * *

I was the conductor of the Underground Railroad for eight years, and I can say what most conductors can't say; I never ran my train off the track, and I never lost a passenger.

* * *

In my dreams and visions, I seemed to see a line, and on the other side of that line were green fields, and lovely flowers, and beautiful white ladies, who stretched out their arms to me over the line, but I couldn't reach them no-how. I always fell before I got to the line.

* * *

I had crossed the line. I was free, but there was no one to welcome me to the land of freedom. I was a stranger in a strange land.

* * *

I grew up like a neglected weed – ignorant of liberty, having no experience of it.

* * *

I've heard 'Uncle Tom's Cabin' read, and I tell you Mrs. Stowe's pen hasn't begun to paint what slavery is as I have seen it at the far South. I've seen de real thing, and I don't want to see it on no stage or in no theater.

* * *

Never wound a snake; kill it.

* * *

I looked at my hands to see if I was the same person. There was such a glory over everything. The sun came up like gold through the trees, and I felt like I was in heaven.

* * *

I would fight for my liberty so long as my strength lasted, and if the time came for me to go, the Lord would let them take me.

* * *

Quakers are almost as good as color. They call themselves friends, and you can trust them every time.

* * *

Wasn't me, 'was the Lord! I always told Him, 'I trust to you. I don't know where to go or what to do, but I expect You to lead me,' an' He always did.

* * *

I said to de Lord, 'I'm groin' to hold steady on to you, an' I know you'll see me through.'

* * *

'Pears like I prayed all the time; 'bout my work, everywhere, I prayed an' groaned to the Lord.

* * *

Most of those coming from the mainland are very destitute, almost naked. I am trying to find places for those able to work and provide for them as best I can, to lighten the burden on the Government as much as possible, while at the same time they learn to respect themselves by earning their own living.

* * *

As I lay so sick on my bed, from Christmas till March, I was always praying for the poor ole master. 'Pears like I didn't do anything but pray for the ole master. 'Oh, Lord, convert ole master;' 'Oh, dear Lord, change that man's heart, and make him a Christian.'

* * *

Lord, I'm going to hold steady on to You, and You've got to see me through.

* * *

I think there's many a slaveholder will get to Heaven. They don't know better. They act up to the light they have.

* * *

You'll be free or die!

* * *

Read my letter to the old folks, and give my love to them, and tell my brothers to be always watching unto prayer, and when the good old ship of Zion comes along, to be ready to step aboard.

* * *

I can't die but once.

* * *

Pears like my heart go flutter, flutter, and then they may say, 'Peace, Peace,' as much as they like – I know it's goin' to be war!

* * *

Why, der language down dar in de far South is jus' as different from ours in Maryland, as you can think. Dey laughed when dey heard me talk, an' I could not understand 'dem, no how.

HELEN KELLER

Helen Adams Keller (June 27, 1880 – June 1, 1968) was an American author, political activist, and lecturer. She was the first deaf-blind person to earn a bachelor of arts degree. The depictions of the play and film The Miracle Worker made widely known the story of how Keller's teacher, Anne Sullivan, was able to communicate with her and teach Keller to speak. Her birthplace in West Tuscumbia, Alabama, is now a museum and sponsors an annual "Helen Keller Day." Her birthday on June 27 is commemorated as Helen Keller Day in the U.S. state of Pennsylvania and was authorized at the federal level by presidential proclamation by President Jimmy Carter in 1980, the 100th anniversary of her birth.

A prolific author, Keller was well-traveled and outspoken in her convictions. A member of the Socialist Party of America and the Industrial Workers of the World, she campaigned for women's suffrage, labor rights, socialism, antimilitarism, and other similar causes. She was inducted into the Alabama Women's Hall of Fame in 1971 and was one of twelve inaugural inductees to the Alabama Writers Hall of Fame on June 8, 2015.

Imagine a person who couldn't see or hear, but despite this, they could still write, read and make friends. They also went to university, wrote many books, traveled all over the world and met 12 US presidents. What an amazing person that would be! Incredibly, a person like this really existed! Her name was Helen Keller. She was from Alabama in the USA, and she was both blind and deaf.

* * *

One can never consent to creep when one feels the impulse to soar.

* * *

Science may have found a cure for most evils; but it has found no remedy for the worst of them all – the apathy of human beings.

* * *

What we have enjoyed we can never lose. All that we love deeply becomes a part of us.

* * *

Many persons have a wrong idea of what constitutes true happiness. It is not attained through self-gratification, but through fidelity to a worthy purpose.

* * *

The most pathetic person in the world is someone who has sight but has no vision.

* * *

We can do anything we want as long as we stick to it long enough.

* * *

Alone we can do so little; together we can do so much.

* * *

I long to accomplish a great and noble task, but it is my chief duty to accomplish small tasks as if they were great and noble.

* * *

So long as you can sweeten another's pain, life is not in vain.

* * *

When one door of happiness closes, another opens; but often we look so long at the closed door that we do not see the one which has been opened for us.

* * *

Although the world is full of suffering, it is full also of the overcoming of it.

* * *

Keep your face to the sun, and you will never see the shadows.

* * *

Everything has its wonders, even darkness, and silence, and I learn, whatever state I may be in, therein to be content.

* * *

The highest result of education is tolerance.

* * *

Optimism is the faith that leads to achievement. Nothing can be done without hope or confidence.

* * *

I would rather walk with a friend in the dark, than alone in the light.

* * *

The only blind person at Christmas-time is he who has not Christmas in his heart.

* * *

I am only one, but still, I am one. I cannot do everything, but still, I can do something; I will not refuse to do something I can do.

* * *

Until the great mass of the people shall be filled with a sense of responsibility for each other's welfare, social justice can never be attained.

* * *

Faith is the strength by which a shattered world shall emerge into the light.

* * *

Life is an exciting business, and most exciting when it is lived for others.

* * *

So much has been given to me I have not the time to ponder over that which has been denied.

* * *

I do not want the peace that passeth understanding. I want the understanding which bringeth peace.

* * *

Four things to learn in life: To think clearly without hurry or confusion; to love everybody sincerely; to act in everything with the highest motives; to trust God unhesitatingly.

* * *

I believe that God is in me as the sun is in the color and fragrance of a flower – the Light in my darkness, the Voice in my silence.

* * *

I believe in the immortality of the soul because I have within me immortal longings.

* * *

No king has not had a slave among his ancestors, and no slave who has not had a king among his.

* * *

It all comes to this: the simplest way to be happy is to do good.

* * *

It is for us to pray not for tasks equal to our powers, but for powers equal to our tasks, to go forward with a great desire forever beating at the door of our hearts as we travel toward our distant goal.

* * *

I look upon the whole world as my fatherland, and every war has to me the horror of a family feud.

* * *

No one has the right to consume happiness without producing it.

* * *

We differ, blind and seeing, one from another, not in our senses, but in use, we make of them, in the imagination and courage with which we seek wisdom beyond the senses.

* * *

Avoiding danger is no safer in the long run than outright exposure. The fearful are caught as often as the bold.

* * *

The marvelous richness of human experience would lose something of rewarding joy if there were no limitations to overcome. The hilltop hour would not be half so wonderful if there were no dark valleys to traverse.

* * *

There is beauty in everything, even in
silence and darkness.

* * *

No matter how dull, or how mean, or how wise a man
is, he feels that happiness is his indisputable right.

* * *

Life is either a daring adventure or nothing at all.
Security is mostly a superstition. It does not exist in
nature.

* * *

The best and most beautiful things in the world cannot
be seen, nor touched − but are felt in the heart.

* * *

People don't like to think, if one thinks, one must
reach conclusions. Conclusions are not always pleasant.

* * *

College isn't the place to go for ideas.

* * *

We could never learn to be brave and patient if there
were only joys in the world.

* * *

As the eagle was killed by the arrow winged with his own feather, so the hand of the world is wounded by its own skill.

* * *

No pessimist ever discovered the secret of the stars, or sailed to an uncharted land, or opened a new doorway for the human spirit.

* * *

Toleration is the greatest gift of mind; it requires the same effort of the brain that it takes to balance oneself on a bicycle.

* * *

It gives me a deep comforting sense that things seen are temporal and things unseen are eternal.

* * *

A character cannot be developed in ease and quiet. Only through experience of trial and suffering can the soul be strengthened, vision cleared, ambition inspired, and success achieved.

* * *

People don't like to think, if one thinks, one must reach conclusions. Conclusions are not always pleasant.

* * *

You don't love someone for their looks, or their clothes, or for their fancy car, but because they sing a song only you can hear

* * *

The best way out is always through.

* * *

Death is no more than passing from one room into another. But there's a difference for me, you know. Because in that other room I shall be able to see.

* * *

Never bend your head. Hold it high. Look the world straight in the eye.

* * *

It is wonderful how much time good people spend fighting the devil. If they would only expend the same amount of energy loving their fellow men, the devil would die in his own tracks of ennui.

* * *

Tyranny cannot defeat the power of ideas.

* * *

Security is mostly a superstition. It does not exist in nature, nor do the children of men as a whole experience it. Avoiding danger is no safer in the long run than outright exposure. Life is either a daring adventure or nothing.

* * *

Self-pity is our worst enemy, and if we yield to it, we can never do anything good in the world

* * *

Literature is my Utopia.

* * *

For three things I thank God every day of my life: thanks that he has vouchsafed me knowledge of his works; deep thanks that he has set in my darkness the lamp of faith; deep, deepest thanks that I have another life to look forward to – a life joyous with light and flowers and heavenly song.

* * *

If the blind put their hands in God's, they find their way more surely than those who see but have not faith or purpose.

* * *

The best-educated human being is the one who understands most about the life in which he is placed.

* * *

Believe, when you are most unhappy, that there is something for you to do in the world.

* * *

When one reads hurriedly and nervously, having in mind written tests and examinations, one's brain becomes encumbered with a lot of bric-a-brac for which there seems to be little use.

* * *

If we spend the time, we waste in sighing for the perfect golden fruit in fulfilling the conditions of its growth; happiness will come, must come. It is guaranteed in the very laws of the universe. If it involves some chastening and renunciation, well, the fruit will be all the sweeter for this touch of holiness.

* * *

As selfishness and complaint pervert and cloud the mind, so sex with its joy clears and sharpens the vision.

* * *

Unless we form the habit of going to the Bible in bright moments as well as in trouble, we cannot fully respond to its consolations because we lack equilibrium between light and darkness.

* * *

A happy life consists not in the absence, but in the mastery of hardships.

* * *

Blindness separates people from things; deafness separates people from people.

* * *

There is no better way to thank God for your sight than by giving a helping hand to someone in the dark.

* * *

Our democracy is but a name. We vote. What does that mean? It means that we choose between two bodies of real – though not avowed – autocrats. We choose between Tweedledum and Tweedledee.

* * *

Tolerance is the first principle of the community; it is the spirit which conserves the best that all men think.

* * *

There are no shortcuts to any place worth going.

* * *

Toleration is the greatest gift of the mind; it requires the same effort of the brain that it takes to balance oneself on a bicycle.

* * *

What I'm looking for is not out there, it is in me.

* * *

Be of good cheer. Do not think of today's failures, but of the success that may come tomorrow. You have set yourselves a difficult task, but you will succeed if you persevere, and you will find a joy in overcoming obstacles. Remember, no effort that we make to attain something beautiful is ever lost.

* * *

Happiness is the final and perfect fruit of obedience to the laws of life.

* * *

To keep our faces toward change, and behave like free spirits in the presence of fate, is strength undefeatable.

* * *

Faith is the strength by which a shattered world shall emerge into the light.

* * *

If it is true that the violin is the most perfect of musical instruments, then Greek is the violin of human thought.

* * *

When we do the best that we can, we never know what miracle is wrought in our life, or in the life of another.

* * *

The world is not moved only by the mighty shoves of the heroes, but also by the aggregate of the tiny pushes of each honest worker.

* * *

Once I knew only darkness and stillness. My life was without past or future. But a little word from the fingers of another fell into my hand that clutched at emptiness, and my heart leaped to the rapture of living.

* * *

Life is a succession of lessons which must be lived to be understood

* * *

I wonder what becomes of lost opportunities? Perhaps our guardian angel gathers them up as we drop them, and will give them back to us in the beautiful sometimes when we have grown wiser and learned how to use them rightly.

* * *

The unselfish effort to bring cheer to others will be the beginning of a happier life for ourselves.

* * *

We need limitations and temptations to open our inner selves, dispel our ignorance, tear off disguises, throw down old idols, and destroy false standards. Only by such rude awakenings can we be led to dwell in a place where we are less cramped, less hindered by the ever-insistent External.

* * *

Change: a bend in the road is not the end of the road...
unless you fail to make the turn.

* * *

It is a mistake always to contemplate the good and
ignore the evil because by making people neglectful it
lets in disaster. There is a dangerous optimism of
ignorance and indifference.

* * *

The most beautiful world is always entered through
imagination.

* * *

I thank God for my handicaps. For through them, I
have found myself, my work and my God.

* * *

If I regarded my life from the point of view of the
pessimist, I should be undone. I should seek in vain for
the light that does not visit my eyes and the music that
does not ring in my ears. I should beg night and day and
never be satisfied. I should sit apart in awful solitude, a
prey to fear and despair. But since I consider it a duty to

myself and to others to be happy, I escape a misery worse than any physical deprivation.

* * *

Strike against war, for without you no battles can be fought. Strike against manufacturing shrapnel and gas bombs and all other tools of murder. Strike against preparedness that means death and misery to millions of human beings. Be not dumb, obedient slaves in an army of destruction. Be heroes in an army of construction.

* * *

Face your deficiencies and acknowledge them, but do not let them master you. Let them teach you patience, sweetness, insight.

HILLARY CLINTON

Hillary Clinton (born October 26, 1947) which her decisiveness and intellectual authority has also been acknowledged globally Undoubtedly one of the world's most dynamic and powerful living women, Clinton bided her time as First Lady of the United States during her husband, Bill Clinton's, presidency from 1993 to 2001, before commencing her own political career. The former lawyer moved to New York to stand as a senator in 2000 and rose to become a strong chance in the 2008 presidential nomination race. Barack Obama narrowly beat her, but her strategic talent and leadership potential were recognized with the key foreign-policy role, a position in.

* * *

If a country doesn't recognize minority rights and human rights, including women's rights, you will not have the kind of stability and prosperity that is possible.

* * *

Women are the largest untapped reservoir of talent in the world.

* * *

Do all the good you can, at all the times you can, to all the people you can, as long as ever you can.

* * *

I think the world would be a lot better off if more people were to define themselves in terms of their own standards and values and not what other people said or thought about them.

* * *

Let's continue to stand up for those who are vulnerable to being left out or marginalized.

* * *

I believe that the rights of women and girls are the unfinished business of the 21st century. The worst thing that can happen in a democracy — as well as in an individual's life is to become cynical about the future and lose hope.

* * *

Human rights are women's rights, and women's rights are human rights.

* * *

We should remember that just as a positive outlook on life can promote good health, so can everyday acts of kindness.

* * *

There is a sense that things if you keep positive and optimistic about what can be done, do work out.

* * *

I can't stand whining. I can't stand the kind of paralysis that some people fall into because they're not happy with the choices they've made. You live in a time when there are endless choices. ... But you have to work on yourself. ... Do something!

* * *

Dignity does not come from avenging insults, especially from the violence that can never be justified. It comes from taking responsibility and advancing our common humanity.

* * *

I think that if you live long enough, you realize that so much of what happens in life is out of your control, but how you respond to it is in your control. That's what I try to remember.

* * *

You know, everybody has setbacks in their life, and everybody falls short of whatever goals they might set for themselves. That's part of living and coming to terms with who you are as a person.

* * *

If you want to know how strong a country's health system is, look at the well beings of its mothers.

* * *

Take criticism seriously, but not personally. If there is truth or merit in the criticism, try to learn from it. Otherwise, let it roll right off you.

JULIA CHILD

Julia Child (August 15, 1912 - August 13, 2004) was an American chef, author, and television personality. She is recognized for bringing French cuisine to the American public with her debut cookbook, Mastering the Art of French Cooking, and her subsequent television programs, the most notable of which was The French Chef, which premiered in 1963.

* * *

How can a nation be called great if its bread tastes like Kleenex?

* * *

You find yourself refreshed by the presence of cheerful people. Why not make an honest effort to confer that pleasure on others? Half the battle is gained if you never allow yourself to say anything gloomy.

* * *

Noncooks think it's silly to invest two hours' work in two minutes' enjoyment; but if cooking is evanescent, so is the ballet.

* * *

Life itself is the proper binge.

* * *

Personally, I don't think pure vegetarianism is a healthy lifestyle. I've often wondered to myself: Does a vegetarian look forward to dinner, ever?

* * *

Moderation. Small helpings. Sample a little bit of everything. These are the secrets of happiness and good health.

* * *

If you're in a good profession, it's hard to get bored, because you're never finished. There will always be work you haven't done.

* * *

Find something you're passionate about and keep tremendously interested in it.

* * *

The measure of achievement is not winning awards. It's doing something that you appreciate, something you believe is worthwhile. I think of my strawberry souffle. I did that at least 28 times before I finally conquered it.

* * *

Drama is very important in life: You have to come on with a bang! You never want to go out with a whimper.

* * *

I enjoy cooking with wine; sometimes I even put it in the food I'm cooking.

* * *

Dining with one's friends and beloved family is certainly one of life's primal and most innocent delights, one that is both soul-satisfying and eternal.

* * *

Always start out with a larger pot than what you think you need.

* * *

Celebrity has its uses. I can always get a seat in any restaurant.

* * *

I find that if I just taste everything and eat small portions, I maintain my weight. I watch my fat intake, but I eat hearty.

* * *

Tears mess up your make-up.

* * *

Remember, no one's more important than people! In other words, friendship is the most important thing. Not career or housework, or one's fatigue; and it needs to be tended and nurtured.

* * *

In department stores, so much kitchen equipment is bought indiscriminately by people who just come in for men's underwear.

* * *

Fat gives things flavor.

* * *

Just like becoming an expert in wine – you learn by drinking it, the best you can afford – you learn about great food by finding the best there is, whether simply or luxurious. Then you savor it, analyze it, and discuss it with your companions, and you compare it with other experiences.

* * *

I was 32 when I started cooking; up until then, I just ate.

* * *

Some people like to paint pictures, or do gardening, or build a boat in the basement. Other people get a tremendous pleasure out of the kitchen because cooking is just as creative and imaginative an activity as drawing, or wood carving, or music.

* * *

In France, cooking is a serious art form and a national sport.

* * *

The secret of a happy marriage is finding the right person. You know they're right if you love to be with them all of the time.

* * *

You'll never know everything about anything, especially something you love.

* * *

You don't have to cook fancy or complicated masterpieces – just good food from fresh ingredients.

* * *

The only time to eat diet food is while you're waiting for the steak to cook.

* * *

In spite of food fads, fitness programs, and health concerns, we must never lose sight of a beautifully conceived meal.

* * *

Being tall is an advantage, especially in business. People will always remember you. And if you're in a crowd, you'll always have some clean air to breathe.

* * *

No one is born a great cook; one learns by doing.

* * *

It's fun to get together and have something good to eat at least once a day. That's what human life is all about – enjoying things.
If you're afraid of butter, use cream.

* * *

This is my invariable advice to people: Learn how to cook, try new recipes, learn from your mistakes, be fearless, and above all – have fun!

* * *

Noelle cuisine is so beautifully arranged on the plate – you know someone's fingers have been all over it.

* * *

The best way to execute French cooking is to get good and loaded and whack the hell out of a chicken.
Bon appetite.

* * *

I think every woman should have a blowtorch.

* * *

I don't think about whether people will remember me or not. I've been an okay person. I've learned a lot. I've taught people a thing or two. That's what's important. A cookbook is only as good as its worst recipe.

* * *

Always remember: If you're alone in the kitchen and you drop the lamb, you can always just pick it up. Who's going to know?

I just hate health food.

JOAN CRAWFORD

Joan Crawford (March 23, c. 1904 - May 10, 1977) was an American actress who began her career as a dancer and stage showgirl. In 1999, the American Film Institute ranked Crawford tenth on its list of the greatest female stars of Classic Hollywood Cinema.

Beginning her career as a dancer in traveling theatrical companies before debuting as a chorus girl on Broadway, Crawford signed a motion picture contract with Metro-Goldwyn-Mayer in 1925. In the 1930s, Crawford's fame rivaled, and later outlasted, that of MGM colleagues Norma Shearer and Greta Garbo. Crawford often played hardworking young women who find romance and success. These characters and stories were well received by Depression-era audiences and were popular with women. Crawford became one of Hollywood's most prominent movie stars, and one of the highest-paid women in the United States, but her films began losing money, and, by the end of the 1930s, she was labeled "box office poison." However, her career gradually improved in the early 1940s, and she made a major comeback in 1945 by starring in Mildred Pierce, for which she won the Academy Award for Best Actress.

* * *

Don't fuck with me, fellas. This cowgirl has been to the rodeo before.

* * *

Working with Bette Davis on Whatever Happened to Baby Jane was one of the greatest challenges I ever had. And I mean that kindly. Bette is of a different temperament than I. Bette had to scream and yell every morning. I just sat and knitted. I knitted a scarf from Hollywood to Malibu.

* * *

You have to be self-reliant and strong to survive in this town. Otherwise, you will be destroyed.

* * *

I love playing bitches. There's a lot of bitch in every woman – a lot in every man.

* * *

Love is a fire. But whether it is going to warm your hearth or burn down your house, you can never tell.

* * *

Any actress who appears in public without being well-groomed is digging her own grave.

* * *

Hollywood is like life. You face it with the total of your equipment.

* * *

I want to think every director I've worked with has fallen in love with me.

* * *

Find your own style and have the courage to stick to it.

* * *

Choose your clothes for your way of life.

* * *

Make your wardrobe as versatile as an actress. It should be able to play many roles.
Find your happiest colors – the ones that make you feel good.

* * *

Care for your clothes, like the good friends they are!

* * *

I have always known what I wanted, and that was beauty... in every form

* * *

If you've earned a position, be proud of it. Don't hide it. I want to be recognized. When I hear people say, There's – Joan Crawford! I turn around and say, Hi! How are you?

* * *

I was born in front of a camera and really didn't know anything else.

* * *

If I can't be me, I don't want to be anybody.

* * *

I never go outside unless I look like – Joan Crawford the movie star. If you want to see the girl next door, go next door.

* * *

Send me flowers while I'm alive. They won't do me a damn bit of good when I'm dead.

* * *

I think that the most important thing a woman can have – next to talent, of course – is her hairdresser.

* * *

It has been said that on screen I personified the American woman.

* * *

There was a saying around MGM – Norma Shearer got the productions, Greta Garbo supplied the art, and – Joan Crawford made money to pay for both.

* * *

I believe in the dollar. Everything I earn, I spend!

* * *

I need sex for a clear complexion, but I'd rather do it for love.

* * *

The Democratic party is one that I've always observed. I have struggled greatly in life from the day I was born, and I am honored to be a part of something that focuses on working-class citizens and molds them into a proud specimen. Mr. Roosevelt and Mr. Kennedy have done so much in that regard for the two generations they've won over during their career course.

JOAN RIVERS

Joan Alexandra Molinsky, known professionally as Joan Rivers (June 8, 1933 — September 4, 2014), was an American comedian, actress, writer, producer, and television host. She was noted for her often controversial comedic persona—heavily self-deprecating or sharply acerbic, especially toward celebrities and politicians. In 1986, with her own rival program, The Late Show with Joan Rivers, Rivers became the first woman to host a late-night network television talk show. She subsequently hosted The Joan Rivers Show (1989–1993), winning a Daytime Emmy for Outstanding Talk Show Host. She was nominated in 1984 for a Grammy Award for her album What Becomes a Semi-Legend Most? And was nominated in 1994 for the Tony Award for Best Actress in a Play for her performance of the title role in Sally Marr...and Her Escorts. In 2015, Rivers posthumously received a Grammy Award for Best Spoken Word Album for her book, Diary of a Mad Diva

* * *

I bought a pedigree dog for 300$. My friend said, give me 300$, and I'll shit on your carpet.

* * *

I knew I was an unwanted baby when I saw that my bath toys were a toaster and a radio.

* * *

I once dated a guy who was so dumb; he couldn't count to twenty-one unless he was naked.

* * *

He said I don't want to wake you up.

* * *

I'm Jewish. I don't work out. If God wanted us to bend over, he'd put diamonds on the floor.

* * *

I have so little sex appeal my gynecologist calls me sir.

* * *

The first time I see a jogger smiling, I'll consider it.

* * *

Don't cook. Don't clean. No man will ever make love to a woman because she waxed the linoleum. My God, the floor's immaculate! Lie down, you hot bitch.

* * *

Mick Jagger could French-kiss a moose. He has child-bearing lips.

* * *

Madonna is so hairy – when she lifted her arm, I thought it was Tina Turner in her armpit.

* * *

All my mother told me about sex was that the man goes on top and the woman on the bottom. For three years my husband and I slept in bunk beds.

* * *

I said to my mother-in-law, my house is your house. She said, Get the hell off my property.

* * *

I was so flat I used to put Xs on my chest and write, You are here. I wore angora sweaters just so the guys would have something to pet.

* * *

I said to my husband, my boobs have gone, my stomach's gone, say something nice about my legs. He said Blue goes with everything.

* * *

It's been so long since I made love, I can't remember who gets tied up.

* * *

I like colonic irrigation because sometimes you find old jewelry.

* * *

When a man has a birthday, he takes a day off. When a woman has a birthday, she takes at least three years off.

* * *

Is she fat? Her favorite food is seconds.

* * *

– Come on, Joan, tell us which husband was the best lover? – Yours. – Joan Rivers, Joan Collins

* * *

I hate housework. You make the beds, you do the dishes, and six months later, you have to start all over again.

* * *

The only time a woman has a true orgasm is when she is shopping.

* * *

Anger is a symptom, a way of cloaking and expressing feelings too awful to experience directly – hurt, bitterness, grief and, most of all, fear.

* * *

The nice thing about Viagra is that they are proving men can go blind on it, so you can gain weight and have a great sex life.

* * *

I was the last girl in Larchmont, NY to get married. My mother had a sign-up Last Girl Before Freeway.

* * *

My sex life is so bad; my G-spot has been declared a historical landmark.

* * *

When I saw her sex tape, all I could think of were Paris Hilton's poor parents. The shame, the shame of the Hilton family. To have your daughter do a porno film... in a Marriott hotel.

* * *

I met Adele! What's her song, Rolling in The Deep? She should add fried chicken.

* * *

Don't cook. Don't clean. No man will ever make love to a woman because she waxed the Linoleum. My God, the floor's immaculate! Lie down, you hot bitch.

* * *

No man ever stuck his hand up your dress looking for a library ticket.

* * *

I wish I had a twin so I could know what I'd look like without plastic surgery.

* * *

My daughter and I are very close. We speak every single day, and I call her every day, and I say the same thing, Pick up, I know you're there. And she says the same thing back, How'd you get this new number?

* * *

A friend of mine confused her Valium with her birth control pills. She had 14 kids but didn't give a shit.

* * *

Taking advice about marriage from Elizabeth Taylor is like taking sailing lessons from the captain of the Titanic.

* * *

I was dating a transvestite. My mother said, Marry him. You'll double your wardrobe.

* * *

I have so little sex appeal my gynecologist examines me by telephone.

* * *

A man can sleep around, no questions asked. But if a woman makes 19 or 20 mistakes, she's a tramp.

* * *

My love life is like a piece of Swiss cheese. Most of it's missing, and what's there stinks.

* * *

I've worked with Angelina Jolie. She saw a sign that said Wet Floor one time, and she did.

* * *

Don't tell your kids you had an easy birth or they won't respect you. For years I used to wake up my daughter and say, Melissa, you ripped me to shreds. Now go back to sleep.

* * *

My best birth control now is just to leave the lights on.

* * *

People say that money is not the key to happiness, but I always figured if you have enough money, you can have a key made.

* * *

Bo Derek is so stupid she returns bowling balls because they've got holes in them.
A child of one can be taught not to do certain things such as touch a hot stove, turn on the gas, pull lamps off their tables by their cords, or wake mommy before noon.

* * *

Thank God we're living in a country where the sky's the limit, the stores are open late and you can shop in bed thanks to television.

* * *

I was just reading about the new Lindsay Lohan diet, which is all liquid. 80 proof.

* * *

Elizabeth Taylor was so fat that whenever she went to London in a red dress, 30 passengers would try to board her.

* * *

I have no sex appeal, which kills me. The only way I can ever hear heavy breathing from my husband's side of the bed is when he's having an asthma attack.

* * *

Do you want to get Cindy Crawford confused? Ask her to spell mom backward.

* * *

When you first get married, they open the car door for you. Eighteen years now... once he opened the car door for me in the last four years – we were on the freeway at the time.

* * *

If Kate Winslet had dropped a few pounds, the Titanic would never have sunk.

* * *

The whole Michael Jackson thing was my fault. I told him to date only 28-year-olds. Who knew he would find 20 of them?

* * *

It takes a lot of experience for a girl to kiss like a beginner.

* * *

My face has been tucked in more times than a bedsheet at the Holiday Inn.

* * *

No-one says this, but the vagina drops. I looked down a few years ago and thought, why am I wearing a bunny slipper?

* * *

Don't talk to me about Valentine's Day. At my age, an affair of the heart is a bypass.!

* * *

I've had so much plastic surgery; when I die, they will donate my body to Tupperware.

* * *

I have no sex appeal. I have to blindfold my vibrator.

* * *

Two's a company. Three's fifty bucks.

* * *

Trust your husband, adore your husband, and get as much as you can in your own name.

* * *

Marie Osmond is so pure; not even Moses could part her knees.

* * *

I had a cold, and my doctor recommended coffee enemas. I can never go back to Starbucks.

* * *

Angelina said to me the other night, If I can make one person happy, Joan, I die content. I said, Easy. Give Jennifer Aniston back her husband.

JOANNE ROWLING

Joanne Rowling is writing under the pen names J. K. Rowling and Robert Galbraith (born 31 July 1965), is a British novelist, philanthropist, film producer, television producer, and screenwriter, best known for writing the Harry Potter fantasy series. The books have won multiple awards, and sold more than 500 million copies, becoming the best-selling book series in history. They have also been the basis for a film series, over which Rowling had overall approval on the scripts and was a producer on the final films in the series.

In October 2010, Rowling was named the "Most Influential Woman in Britain" by leading magazine editors. She has supported charities, including Comic Relief, One Parent Families and Multiple Sclerosis Society of Great Britain, and launched her own charity, Lumos.

* * *

If you want to know what a man's like, take a good look at how he treats his inferiors, not his equals

* * *

I was set free because my greatest fear had been realized, and I still had a daughter who I adored, and I had an old typewriter and a big idea. And so rock bottom became a solid foundation on which I rebuilt my life.

* * *

The truth. It is a beautiful and terrible thing, and must, therefore, be treated with great caution.

* * *

Failure is not fun. It can be awful. But living so cautiously that you never fail is worse.

* * *

Talent and intelligence never yet inoculated anyone against the caprice of the fates.

* * *

You are the true master of death because the true master does not seek to run away from Death. He accepts that he must die, and understands that there are far, far worse things in the living world than dying.

* * *

It matters not what someone is born, but what they grow to be.

* * *

It is our choices...that show what we truly are, far more than our abilities.

* * *

You sort of start thinking anything is possible if
you've got enough nerve.
It takes a great deal of bravery to stand up to our
enemies, but just as much to stand up to our friends.

* * *

If someone asked for my recipe for happiness, step
one would be finding out what you love doing the most
in the world and step two would be finding someone to
pay you to do it.

* * *

We can choose. Things go largely like you want them
to go. You control your own life. Your own will is
extremely powerful.
Indifference and neglect often do much more damage
than outright dislike.

* * *

It does not do to dwell on dreams and forget to live.

* * *

We've all got both light and dark inside us. What
matters is the part we choose to act on. That's who we
really are.

* * *

People find it far easier to forgive others for being wrong than being right.

* * *

Failure means a stripping away of the inessential.

* * *

Happiness can be found, even in the darkest of times, if one only remembers to turn on the light.

* * *

As is a tale, so is life: not how long it is, but how good it is, is what matters.

* * *

To the well-organized mind, death is but the next great adventure.

* * *

Never be ashamed! There's some who'll hold it against you, but they're not worth bothering with.

* * *

Is 'fat' really the worse thing a human being can be?
Is 'fat' worse than 'vindictive,' 'jealous,' 'shallow,'
'vain,' 'boring,' or 'cruel'? Not to me.

* * *

Whatever money you might have, self-worth really
lies in finding out what you do best.

* * *

You will never truly know yourself, or the strength of
your relationships until both have been tested by
adversity.

* * *

We have to choose between what is right,
and what is easy.

* * *

Fear of a name increases fear of the thing itself.

* * *

We do not need magic to transform our world. We
carry all of the power we need inside ourselves already.

* * *

Failure is so important. We speak about success all the time. It is the ability to resist failure or use failure that often leads to greater success. I've met people who don't want to try for fear of failing.

* * *

You've got to work. It's about structure. It's about discipline. It's all these deadly things that your schoolteacher told you needed...you need it.

* * *

I think you have a moral responsibility when you've been given far more than you need, to do wise things with it and give intelligently.

* * *

What's coming will come, and we'll just have to meet it when it does.

***

It is impossible to live without failing at something unless you live so cautiously that you might as well not have lived at all, in which case you have failed by default.

* * *

I would like to be remembered as someone who did the best she could with the talent she had.

* * *

Life is difficult and complicated, and beyond anyone's total control, and the humility to know that will enable you to survive its vicissitudes.

* * *

The knowledge that you have emerged wiser and stronger from setbacks means that you are, ever after, secure in your ability to survive.

* * *

The consequences of our actions are always so complicated, so diverse, that predicting the future is a very difficult business indeed.

ELIZABETH ARDEN

Elizabeth Arden was the founder, owner, and operator of Elizabeth Arden, Inc., a cosmetics and beauty corporation. She used modern mass marketing techniques to bring her cosmetic products to the public, committed to an approach that emphasized natural beauty. Her slogan was To be beautiful and natural is the birthright of every woman. She also opened and operated a chain of beauty salons and beauty spas. She was also noted for her passion for owning racehorses; a horse from one of her stables won the Kentucky Derby in 1947. She lived from December 31, 1884 - October 18, 1966. Her cosmetics and beauty products brand continues today.

* * *

It was the beginning of my real life,
my coming of age...

* * *

I vowed myself then and there to nature...

* * *

I... have been happy ever since.

* * *

Every skin requires an astringent tonic and a nourishing cream.

* * *

Keep it exquisitely clean.

* * *

Learn not to over-massage...

* * *

No one method of treatment sets the same with all persons...

* * *

Quest of the beautiful.

* * *

This business is... essentially feminine. What male executive will throw away a whole batch of powder, because the shade's off an indiscernible fraction? Or spend weeks mixing nail polish to get the right color – the one woman will adore? I've been doing it every day of my life. Everybody copies me.

* * *

I'm not interested in age. People who tell me their age are silly. You're as old as you feel.

* * *

Hold fast to life and youth.

* * *

Nothing that costs only a dollar is worth having.

* * *

Repetition makes reputation and reputation make customers.

* * *

I don't want them [staff] to love me, I want them to fear me.

* * *

[On the 1929 Wall Street Crash] Our clients are coping with the stress of financial loss by soaking in a hot bath scented with my Rose Geranium bath crystals.

* * *

I found I didn't really like looking at sick people. I want to keep people well, and young, and beautiful.

* * *

[In 1959 when she was told one of her racehorses had bitten off the tip of a person's finger] What happened to the horse?

* * *

[On passing by a limestone façade bearing the words 'Helena Rubinstein' after she had passed three weeks earlier at the age of 94] Poor Helena. [Elizabeth herself passed away just 18 months later at the age of 81]

* * *

When people think pink... they think Arden.

* * *

[At a political fundraiser towards the end of the 1930s] You don't have to do anything, my dears – just vote Republican.

* * *

[During the depression] Women are cheered by makeup. When the moneyed spend less on clothes, they spend more on lipstick.

* * *

Do you want your makeup to stay on for hours and hours?

* * *

Do you want something that will help keep a blemish out of sight?

* * *

Do you want your skin to glow through your powder?

* * *

Do you want to help hide your freckles?

* * *

You're in another world... when you come through the red door of Elizabeth Arden. And the world is based on one exclusive object – you. Whatever your need or the time you have on your hands.

* * *

[To her skeptical father] I am going to make us rich just as soon as I perfect my beauty cream.

* * *

Before you start off anything, why don't you start of with a clean slate.

* * *

Beautiful gives her daughter something to look forward to.

* * *

Beautiful stands the test of time.

* * *

Beautiful is knowing you are one of a kind.

* * *

Beautiful never looks back.

* * *

Some people feel the rain. Others just get wet. Be true to who you are.

* * *

Beautiful blossoms in every season.

* * *

I rarely hire anyone who is out of a job.

* * *

I pick good women, but I haven't had any luck with my men.

[On Helena Rubinstein] That woman.

* * *

[On reading 'Elizabeth and Her German Garden' – It] Brought back my childhood with a rush and all the happy days I spent in a garden... It was the beginning of my real life, my coming of age as it were, and entering into my kingdom... I vowed myself then and there to nature, and have been happy ever since.

* * *

To have a wholesome skin is to keep it exquisitely clean. Many times the skin is not thoroughly cleaned, and this is the real cause of blackheads and an impure complexion. It must be light and very oily to properly remove all impurities and prevent the pores from becoming clogged.

* * *

My long experience and great success have positively convinced me that every skin requires an astringent tonic and a nourishing cream.

* * *

A woman has always been searching for the Fountain of Youth, when, like the 'Blue Bird,' it is at home, and simply means ten minutes care night and morning.

* * *

To have a wholesome skin is to keep it exquisitely clean. Many times, the skin is not thoroughly cleaned, and this is the real cause of blackheads and an impure complexion. It must be light and very oily to properly remove all impurities and prevent the pores from becoming clogged.

* * *

It is equally important to promote and stimulate the circulation and clear and firm the skin.

* * *

Learn not to over-massage the face which gives a lifeless looking skin.

* * *

A wholesome, healthy skin, if wrongly treated can become gradually shriveled, old and haggard.

* * *

The very best treatment for the face and throat is to firm the lines and muscles by a peculiar patting in of...

* * *

[On Venetian Special Herb Astringent Cream] This particularly potent astringent firms as if by magic.

* * *

Be taught to administer this treatment yourself. It is well worth learning how.

* * *

The great lesson to learn about beauty charms is that no one method of treatment sets the same with all persons.

* * *

[On Venetian Powder V'illusion] A fascinating shade for sunburned faces.

* * *

Prepare your skin for July and August...

* * *

Beauty treatment is not complete without lipstick.

* * *

There's only one Elizabeth like me, and that's the
Queen.

* * *

Go out and make your mark.

* * *

[To her husband (later ex-husband)] Dear, never
forget one little point. It's my business. You just work
here.

* * *

Women invented management.

* * *

Every woman has the right to be beautiful.

* * *

A woman can always look younger than she really is.

* * *

[The single-minded goal that drove her] To be the
richest little woman in the world.

* * *

I only want people around me who can do the impossible.

* * *

Standards should be set by me and not imposed on me.

* * *

To be beautiful is the birthright of every woman.

* * *

It is remarkable what a woman can accomplish with just a little ambition.

* * *

To achieve beauty, a woman must first achieve health.

* * *

A beautiful horse is like a beautiful woman.

* * *

You're as old as you feel.

* * *

I want them to fear me.

* * *

The cosmetics industry is the nastiest business in the world.
I am going to make us rich...

* * *

A woman has always been searching for the Fountain of Youth...

* * *

Do not produce an artificial, unnatural look by doing too much to your skin.

* * *

The quest of the beautiful.
Beauty is one-part nature, and three parts care.

* * *

There is no reason for a woman to lose even one iota of her beauty.

* * *

There are only three American names that are known in every corner of the globe: Singer sewing machines, Coca-Cola and Elizabeth Arden.

* * *

To have a wholesome skin is to keep it exquisitely clean.

* * *

This business is... essentially feminine.

* * *

What male executive will throw away a whole batch of powder, because the shade's off an indiscernible fraction?

* * *

I'm not interested in age.

* * *

People who tell me their age are silly.

* * *

Many times, the skin is not thoroughly cleaned, and this is the real cause of blackheads and an impure complexion.

* * *

I didn't really like looking at sick people.

* * *

I want to keep people well, and young, and beautiful.

* * *

A woman must first achieve health.

* * *

Women are cheered by makeup.

* * *

When the moneyed spend less on clothes, they spend more on lipstick.

* * *

You're in another world...

* * *

Why don't you start off with a clean slate?

* * *

Many women today still have these same old–
fashioned postures.

* * *

Your posture can be made perfect.

* * *

All the happy days I spent in a garden.

ELIZABETH TAYLOR

Elizabeth Taylor (February 27, 1932—March 23, 2011) One of the film's most celebrated stars, Elizabeth Taylor has fashioned a career that's covered more than six decades, accepting roles that have not only showcased her beauty, but her ability to take on emotionally charged characters

* * *

You find out who your real friends are when you're involved in a scandal.

* * *

My mother says I didn't open my eyes for eight days after I was born, but when I did, the

* * *

First thing I saw was an engagement ring. I was hooked.

* * *

The problem with people who have no vices is that generally, you can be pretty sure they're going to have some pretty annoying virtues.

* * *

Big girls need big diamonds.

* * *

I've only slept with the men I've been married to. How many women can make that claim?

* * *

I've always admitted that I'm ruled by my passions.

* * *

I suppose when they reach a certain age some men are afraid to grow up. It seems the older the men get, the younger their new wives get.

* * *

I, along with the critics, have never taken myself very seriously.

* * *

If someone was stupid enough to offer me a million dollars to make a picture, I'm certainly not dumb enough to turn it down.

* * *

That's the trouble with life – crap dialogue and bad lighting.

* * *

Some of my best leading men have been dogs and horses.

* * *

I feel very adventurous. There are so many doors to be opened, and I'm not afraid to look behind them.

* * *

If not to make the world better, what is money for?

* * *

What is a genius? What is a living legend? What is a megastar? Michael Jackson – that's all. And when you think you know him, he gives you more... I think he is one of the finest people to hit this planet, and, in my estimation, he is the true King of Pop, Rock, and Soul.

* * *

I don't think President Bush is doing anything at all about Aids. In fact, I'm not sure he even knows how to spell Aids.

* * *

He is one of the most normal people I know. – Elizabeth Taylor, on Michael Jackson

* * *

Pour yourself a drink, put on some lipstick, and pull yourself together.

* * *

You just do it. You force yourself to get up. You push yourself to put one foot before the other, and God damn it, you refuse to let it get to you. You fight. You cry. You curse. Then you go about the business of living. That's how I've done it. There's no other way.

* * *

I don't pretend to be an ordinary housewife.

* * *

There's still so much more to do. I can't sit back and be complacent, and none of us should be. I get around now in a wheelchair, but I get around.

* * *

Success is a great deodorant. It takes away all your past smells.

* * *

I am a very committed wife. And I should be committed too – for being married so many times.

* * *

I've been married too many times. How terrible to change children's affiliations, their affections – to give them the insecurity of placing their trust in someone when maybe that someone won't be there next year.

* * *

I've been through it all, baby, I'm mother courage.

* * *

I don't entirely approve of some of the things I have done, or am, or have been. But I'm me.

* * *

God knows I'm me.

* * *

The most gorgeous thing in the world and easily one of the best actors.

* * *

The ups and downs, the problems and stress, along with all the happiness, have given me optimism and hope because I am living proof of survival.

* * *

I think I'm finally growing up – and about time. – Elizabeth Taylor, on turning 53 years old

* * *

He is as tough as an old nut and as soft as a yellow ribbon. – Elizabeth Taylor, on John Wayne

* * *

When people say: She's got everything. I've only one answer: I haven't had tomorrow.

* * *

When you are fat, the world; is divided into two groups – people who bug you and people who leave you alone.

The funny thing is, supporters and saboteurs exist in either camp.

* * *

It's not the having, it's the getting.

* * *

I had a hollow leg. I could drink everyone under the table and not get drunk. My capacity was terrifying.

* * *

I fell off my pink cloud with a thud.

* * *

I have the emotions of a child in the body of a woman. I was rushed into womanhood for the movies. It caused me long moments of unhappiness and doubt.

* * *

I sweat real sweat, and I shake real shakes.

* * *

I really don't remember much about Cleopatra. There were a lot of other things going on.

* * *

I adore wearing gems, but not because they are mine.
You can't possess radiance; you can only admire it.

ELLEN DEGENERES

Ellen DeGeneres (born January 26, 1958) is an American comedian, television host, actress, writer, producer, and LGBT activist. She starred in the popular sitcom Ellen from 1994 to 1998 and has hosted her syndicated TV talk show, The Ellen DeGeneres Show, since 2003.

Her stand-up career started in the early 1980s and included a 1986 appearance on The Tonight Show Starring Johnny Carson. As a film actress, DeGeneres starred in Mr. Wrong(1996), EDtv (1999), and The Love Letter (1999), and provided the voice of Dory in the Pixar animated films Finding Nemo (2003) and Finding Dory (2016); for Nemo, she was awarded the Saturn Award for Best Supporting Actress, the first time an actress won a Saturn Award for a voice performance. In 2010, she was a judge on American Idol for its ninth season.

She starred in two television sitcoms, Ellen from 1994 to 1998, and The Ellen Show from 2001 to 2002. During the fourth season of Ellen in 1997, she came out as a lesbian in an appearance on The Oprah Winfrey Show. Her character, Ellen Morgan, also came out to a therapist played by Winfrey, and the series went on to explore various LGBT issues, including the coming-out process. This made her the first openly lesbian actress to play an openly lesbian character on television. In 2008, she married her longtime girlfriend, Portia de Rossi.

DeGeneres has hosted the Academy Awards, Grammy

Awards, and the Primetime Emmys. She has authored four books and started her own record company Eleveneleven, as well as a production company, A Very Good Production. She also launched a lifestyle brand, ED Ellen DeGeneres, which comprises a collection of apparel, accessories, home, baby, and pet items. She has won 30 Emmys, 20 People's Choice Awards (more than any other person), and numerous other awards for her work and charitable efforts. In 2016, she received the Presidential Medal of Freedom.

* * *

In the beginning, there was nothing. God said, let there be light! And there was light. There was still nothing, but you could see it a whole lot better.

* * *

Because you can't rely on other people, for your own ego you need daily affirmations. Some obvious affirmations are: I am a good person. or I love myself or I matter. But I think it's a good idea to start small. You should say things that make you feel good because they are easy to accomplish. (I will wake up. I will brush my teeth.) Don't push yourself. Those can be very good morning affirmations. I guess, though, if you're really depressed, and it's 8 o'clock at night, I will wake up would technically be an evening affirmation.

* * *

You can put high heels on a poodle, but that won't make it a hooker.

* * *

My friend's dog has a sweater, but he wears it wrapped around his shoulders.

* * *

We're told to go on living our lives as usual, because to do otherwise is to let the terrorists win, and really, what would upset the Taliban more than a gay woman wearing a suit in front of a room full of Jews?

* * *

I don't need a baby growing inside of me for nine months, either. For one thing, there's morning sickness. If I'm going to feel nauseous and achy when I wake up, I want to achieve that state the old-fashioned way: getting good and drunk the night before.

* * *

My favorite exercise is walking a block and a half to buy fudge. Then I call a cab to get me home. There's never a need to overdo anything.

* * *

– So, what should we call you, gay or lesbian? – How about Ellen?
You can always tell when the relationship is over. Little things start grating on your nerves.

* * *

Would you please stop that! That breathing in and out, it's so repetitious!

* * *

Normal is getting dressed in clothes that you buy for work and driving through traffic in a car that you are still paying for – in order to get to the job you need to pay for the clothes and the car, and the house you leave vacant all day so you can afford to live in it.

* * *

My grandmother started walking five miles a day when she was sixty. She's ninety-seven now, and we don't know where the heck she is.

* * *

Stuffed deer heads on walls are bad enough, but it's worse when they are wearing dark glasses, and have streamers in their antlers because then you know they were enjoying themselves at a party when they were shot.

* * *

I feel extremely lucky to have my own TV show. Every day I pinch myself because I'm sure I must be dreaming. Actually, I don't pinch myself. It's one of my manager's jobs to pinch me and say, You aren't dreaming', kid! Then I pinch him, he pinches me back, and it usually ends up in a slap fight. Sometimes the slap fight lasts until midnight.

* * *

I wonder what will happen if I put hand cream on my feet, will they get confused and start clapping?

* * *

The only thing that scares me more than space aliens is the idea that there aren't any space aliens. We can't be the best that creation has to offer. I pray we're not all there is. If so, we're in big trouble.

* * *

Do things that make you happy within the confines of the legal system.

* * *

Hey, Debbie, this is Ellen. That's a really cute phone message. You sounded just like Elmer Fudd. Geez, I hope

you were trying to sound like Elmer Fudd. If you weren't, I'm terribly sorry. Thanks for saying that you'd watch my house while I'm gone next week on vacation to the Luxembourg Soft Cheese and Jazz Festival. I know you said you would water the plants, bring in the mail and turn some lights on so that it looks like somebody is home. But if it's not too much of an imposition, could you also make sure that the mobile over the crib isn't tangled? Otherwise, the baby is just going to get bored. I never knew to have a kid was so much responsibility!
Bye–bye.

* * *

Do we have to know who's gay and who's straight? Can't we just love everybody and judge them by the car they drive?

* * *

Accept who you are. Unless you're a serial killer. I don't have a type. It took me this long to narrow it down to gender.

* * *

I have to wear pants. I had both of my legs tattooed all over with designs of bougainvillea. Now, if I wear a skirt, I am constantly bothered by bees.
We used to have a fire drill practice in my house. Everyone had their own special duty. My dad had to get

the pets; my mom took the jewelry, my brother ran to get help. They told me to save the washer and dryer.

* * *

I have a terrible problem with procrastination... a friend told me, Well, you should go to therapy. And I thought about it, but then I said, Wait a minute. Why should I pay a stranger to listen to me talk when I can get strangers to pay to listen to me talk? And that's when I got the idea of touring.

* * *

We always do this: we walk up to an elevator, someone's already there, they're waiting, they've pushed the button, the button is lit. We walk up and push the button, thinking. Obviously you didn't push it correctly. I'll have to push it myself. NOW the elevator will come. Then someone else walks up, and they push the button again. Suddenly you're offended. You want to say, You idiot, I pushed it, he pushed it. Then, to the original pusher, can you believe people?

* * *

All the commercials on TV today are for antidepressants, for Prozac or Paxil. And they get you right away. Are you sad? Do you get stressed, do you have anxiety? Yes, I have all those things! I'm alive!

* * *

Here are the values that I stand for: honesty, equality, kindness, compassion, treating people the way you want to be treated and helping those in need. To me, those are traditional values.

* * *

My point is, life is about balance. The good and the bad. The highs and the lows. The pina and the colada.

* * *

When I'm on a plane, I can never get my seat to recline more than a couple of centimeters, but the guy in front of me – his seat comes back far enough for me to do dental work on him.

* * *

It makes a big difference in your life when you stay positive.

* * *

For a long time, I thought I knew for sure who I was. I grew up in New Orleans and became a comedian. And there was everything that came along with that. The nightclubs. Smoking.
The drinking. Then I turned 13.

If you want to test cosmetics, why do it on some poor animal who hasn't done anything wrong? They should use prisoners who have been convicted of murder or rape instead. So, rather than seeing if some perfume irritates a bunny rabbit's eyes, they should throw it in Charles Manson's eyes and ask him if it hurts.

* * *

Procrastinate now, don't put it off.

* * *

I ask people why they have deer heads on their walls. They always say because it's such a beautiful animal. There you go. I think my mother is attractive, but I have photographs of her.

* * *

I learned compassion from being discriminated against. Everything bad that's ever happened to me has taught me compassion.

* * *

I'll see stray dogs wandering in front of houses, and they look so sad. I just feel compelled to do something to rescue them. Sometimes it's hard because they're tied on a leash on someone's front lawn, so you've got to untie it. Or worse, they're behind a fence, so you need wire cutters (which I always have in my car) to get them out. C'mon, girl. I'll rescue you and find your owners.

* * *

Sometimes you can't see yourself clearly until you see yourself through the eyes of others.

* * *

Our flaws are what makes us human. If we can accept them as part of who we are, they really don't even have to be an issue.

* * *

Penguins mate for life. Which doesn't exactly surprise me that much cause they all look alike – it's not like they're going to meet a better-looking penguin someday.

* * *

Have you ever heard somebody sing some lyrics that you've never sung before, and you realize you've never sung the right words in that song? You hear them and all of a sudden you say to yourself, Life in the Fast Lane? That's what they're saying right there? You think, why have I been singing 'wipe in the Vaseline? How many people have heard me sing wipe in the Vaseline? I am an idiot!

* * *

People always ask me, Were you funny as a child? Well, no, I was an accountant.

* * *

It's our challenges and obstacles that give us layers of depth and make us interesting. Are they fun when they happen? No. But they are what make us unique. And that's what I know for sure... I think.

* * *

The thing everyone should realize is that the key to happiness is being happy for yourself and yourself.

* * *

When you take risks, you learn that there will be times when you succeed, and there will be times when you fail, and both are equally important.

* * *

Our attention span is shot. We've all got Attention Deficit Disorder or ADD or OCD or one of these disorders with three letters because we don't have the time or patience to pronounce the entire disorder. That should be a disorder right there, TBD – Too Busy Disorder.

* * *

Take a nap in a fireplace, and you'll sleep like a log.

* * *

Don't you hate when people are late to work? And they always have the worst excuses. Oh, I'm sorry I'm late, traffic. Traffic, huh? How do you think I got here; helicoptered in?

* * *

In Hollywood, children don't wear masks on Halloween. Instead, they usually dress up as agents, valet parkers, or second-unit directors.

* * *

I'm a godmother, that's a great thing to be, a godmother. She calls me god for short, that's cute, I taught her that.

* * *

High heels should be outlawed (at the very least there should be a five-day waiting period before you can buy them). They destroy your feet. It should be mandatory that the Surgeon General print a warning label on high heels as they do on a package of cigarettes (i.e. Warning: These shoes can lead to lower back pain, aching toes, and the illusion that you're taller than you actually are).

* * *

Beauty is about being comfortable in your own skin. It's about knowing and accepting who you are.

* * *

When I was growing up, we had a petting zoo, and a heavy petting zoo – for people who really liked the animals a lot.

* * *

You know, it's hard work to write a book. I can't tell you how many times I really get going on an idea, then my quill breaks. Or I spill ink all over my writing tunic.

* * *

If we don't want to define ourselves by things as superficial as our appearances, we're stuck with the revolting alternative of being judged by our actions, by what we do.

* * *

When you're walking down the street and you think you've spotted your favorite celebrity, but you want to be sure, just remember this rule of thumb: A horse sweats, a man perspires, a woman glows – but only a celebrity twinkles.

* * *

The world is full of a lot of fear and a lot of negativity, and a lot of judgment. I just think people need to start shifting into joy and happiness. As corny as it sounds, we need to make a shift.

* * *

Follow your passion. Stay true to yourself. Never follow someone else's path unless you're in the woods and you're lost, and you see a path. By all means, you should follow that.

* * *

Laugh. Laugh as much as you can. Laugh until you cry. Cry until you laugh. Keep doing it even if people are passing you on the street saying, I can't tell if that person is laughing or crying, but either way, they seem crazy, let's walk faster. Emote. It's okay. It shows you are thinking and feeling.

GLORIA STEINEM

Gloria Steinem (born March 25, 1934) is an American feminist, journalist, and social-political activist who became nationally recognized as a leader and a spokeswoman for the American feminist movement in the late 1960s and early 1970s. Steinem was a columnist for New York magazine and a co-founder of Ms. Magazine.

In 1969, Steinem published an article, "After Black Power, Women's Liberation," which brought her to national fame as a feminist leader. Gloria Steinem is speaking with supporters at the Women Together Arizona Summit at Carpenters Local Union in Phoenix, Arizona, September 2016.

In 2005, Steinem, Jane Fonda, and Robin Morgan co-founded the Women's Media Center, an organization that works "to make women visible and powerful in the media."

As of May 2018, Steinem travels internationally as an organizer and lecturer and is a media spokeswoman on issues of equality

* * *

A woman reading Playboy feels a little like a Jew reading a Nazi manual.

* * *

The truth will set you free, but first, it will piss you off.

* * *

Any woman who chooses to behave like a full human being should be warned that the armies of the status quo will treat her as something of a dirty joke. That's their natural and first weapon. She will need her sisterhood.

* * *

I have yet to hear a man ask for advice on how to combine marriage and a career.

* * *

Far too many people are looking for the right person, instead of trying to be the right person.

* * *

A feminist is anyone who recognizes the equality and full humanity of women and men.

* * *

If women are supposed to be less rational and more emotional at the beginning of our menstrual cycle when the female hormone is at its lowest level, then why isn't it logical to say that, in those few days, women behave the most like the way men behave all month long?

* * *

A woman without a man is like a fish without a bicycle.

* * *

Once we give up searching for approval, we often find it easier to earn respect.

* * *

We'll never solve the feminization of power until we solve the masculinity of wealth.

* * *

Marriage: A ceremony in which rings are put on the finger of the lady and through the nose of the gentleman.

* * *

Planning ahead is a measure of class. The rich and even the middle-class plan for future generations, but the poor can plan ahead only a few weeks or days.

* * *

Women have two choices: Either she's a feminist or a masochist.

* * *

We've begun to raise daughters more like sons... but few have the courage to raise our sons more like our daughters.

* * *

The first problem for all of us, men and women, is not to learn, but to unlearn.
There are really not many jobs that actually require a penis or a vagina, and all other occupations should be open to everyone.

* * *

One day an army of gray-haired women may quietly take over the Earth.

* * *

God may be in the details, but the goddess is in the questions. Once we begin to ask them, there's no turning back.

* * *

Marriage works best for men than women. The two happiest groups are married men and unmarried women.

* * *

Most American children suffer too much mother and too little father.

* * *

No man can call himself liberal, or radical, or even a conservative advocate of fair play, if his work depends in any way on the unpaid or underpaid labor of women at home, or in the office.

* * *

Clearly, no one knows what leadership has gone undiscovered in women of all races, and in black and other minority men.

* * *

From pacifist to terrorist, each person condemns violence – and then adds one cherished case in which it may be justified

* * *

Most women are one man away from welfare.

* * *

Someone asked me why women don't gamble as much as men do, and I gave the commonsensical reply that we don't have as much money. That was a true and incomplete answer. In fact, women's total instinct for gambling is satisfied by marriage.

* * *

Hope is a very unruly emotion.

* * *

Women may be the one group that grows more radical with age.

* * *

Without leaps of imagination or dreaming, we lose the excitement of possibilities. Dreaming, after all, is a form of planning.

* * *

Most women's magazines simply try to mold women into bigger and better consumers.

* * *

Self-esteem isn't everything; it's just that there's nothing without it.

* * *

Law and justice are not always the same. When they aren't, destroying the law may be the first step toward changing it.

* * *

A woman who aspires to be something is called a bitch.

* * *

Men should think twice before making widowhood women's only path to power.

* * *

This is no simple reform. It really is a revolution. Sex and race because they are easy and visible differences have been the primary ways of organizing human beings into superior and inferior groups and into the cheap labor on which this system still depends. We are talking about a society in which there will be no roles other than those chosen or those earned. We are really talking about humanism.

* * *

We are the women our parents warned us against, and we are proud.

* * *

The authority of any governing institution must stop at its citizen's skin.

* * *

America is an enormous frosted cupcake in the middle of millions of starving people.

* * *

If the shoe doesn't fit, must we change the foot?

* * *

Feminism has never been about getting a job for one woman. It's about making life fairer for women everywhere. It's not about a piece of the existing pie; there are too many of us for that. It's about baking a new pie.

* * *

I have yet to hear a man ask for advice on how to combine marriage and a career.

* * *

But the problem is that when I go around and speak on campuses, I still don't get young men standing up and saying, how can I combine career and family?

* * *

I always wanted to be a writer. I got into activism just because it needed to be done.

* * *

Childbirth is more admirable than conquest, more amazing than self-defense, and as courageous as either one.

* * *

Don't worry about what you should do; worry about what you can do. Writing is the only thing that when I do it, I don't feel I should be doing something else.

* * *

The family is the basic cell of government: it is where we are trained to believe that we are human beings or that we are chattel, it is where we are trained to see the sex and race divisions and become callous to injustice even if it is done to ourselves, to accept as biological a full system of authoritarian government.

* * *

Pornography is instruction. Rape is the practice, battered women are the practice, and battered children are the practice.

* * *

The first resistance to social change is to say it's not necessary.

* * *

I have met brave women who are exploring the outer edge of possibility, with no history to guide them and courage to make themselves vulnerable that I find moving beyond the words to express it.

* * *

Women are always saying. We can do anything that men can do. But Men should be saying. We can do anything that women can do.

* * *

Rich people plan for three generations. Poor people plan for Saturday night.

* * *

A pedestal is as much a prison as any small, confined space.

* * *

Power can be taken, but not given. The process of the taking is empowerment in itself.

* * *

For women... bras, panties, bathing suits, and other stereotypical gear are visual reminders of a commercial, idealized feminine image that our real and diverse female bodies can't possibly fit. Without these visual references, each individual woman's body demands to be accepted on its own terms. We stop being comparatives. We begin to be unique.

* * *

We can tell our values by looking at our checkbook stubs.

* * *

It is more rewarding to watch money change the world than watch it accumulate.

* * *

The future depends entirely on what each of us does every day; a movement is only people moving.

* * *

However sugarcoated and ambiguous, every form of authoritarianism must start with a belief in some group's greater right to power, whether that right is justified by sex, race, class, religion or all four. However far it may expand, the progression inevitably rests on unequal power and airtight roles within the family

* * *

So whatever you want to do, just do it... making a damn fool of yourself is absolutely essential.

* * *

A liberated woman is one who has sex before marriage and a job after.

* * *

Women are not going to be equal outside the home until men are equal in it.

KATHERINE MANSFIELD

Kathleen Mansfield Murry (14 October 1888 − 9 January 1923) was a prominent New Zealand modernist short story writer who was born and brought up in colonial New Zealand and wrote under the pen name of Katherine Mansfield. At 19, Mansfield left New Zealand and settled in England, where she became a friend of writers such as D.H. Lawrence and Virginia Woolf. In 1917, she was diagnosed with extrapulmonary tuberculosis, which led to her death at age 34.

* * *

We can do whatever we wish to do provided our wish is strong enough. What do you want most to do? That's what I have to keep asking myself, in the face of difficulties.

* * *

Risk! Risk anything! Care no more for the opinions of others, for those voices. Do the hardest thing on earth for you. Act for yourself. Face the truth.

* * *

I have made it a rule of my life never to regret and never to look back. Regret is an appalling waste of energy... you can't build on it; it's only good for wallowing in.

* * *

When we begin to take our failures non-seriously, it means we are ceasing to be afraid of them.

* * *

I adore life. What do all the fools matter and all the stupidity? They do matter, but somehow for me, they cannot touch the body of life. Life is marvelous. I want to be deeply rooted in it – to live – to expand – to breathe in it – to rejoice – to share it. To give and to be asked for love.

* * *

I want, by understanding myself, to understand others. I want to be all that I am capable of becoming.

* * *

The pleasure of all reading is doubled when one lives with another who shares the same books.

* * *

I am going to enjoy life in Paris I know. It is so human, and there is something noble in the city. It is a real city, old and fine and life plays in it for everybody to see.

* * *

I always felt that the great high privilege, relief, and comfort of friendship, was that one had to explain nothing.

* * *

I am treating you as my friend, asking you to share my present minuses in the hope that I can ask you to share my future pluses.

* * *

Could we change our attitude, we should not only see life differently, but life itself would come to be different. Life would undergo a change of appearance because we ourselves had undergone a change of attitude.

* * *

To acknowledge the presence of fear is to give birth to failure.

* * *

I'm a writer first and a woman after.

* * *

Life never becomes a habit to me. It's always a marvel.

* * *

The mind I love must still have wild places, a tangled orchard where dark damsons drop in the heavy grass, an overgrown little wood, the chance of a snake or two, a pool that nobody's fathomed the depth of – and paths threaded with those little flowers planted by the mind.

* * *

I imagine I was always writing. Twaddle it was, too. But better far write twaddle or anything, anything, than nothing at all.

* * *

Were we positive, eager, real – alive? No, we were not. We were a nothingness shot with gleams of what might be.

* * *

If only one could tell true love from false love as one can tell mushrooms from toadstools!

* * *

Everything in life that we really accept undergoes a change. So, suffering must become love. That is the mystery.

* * *

Would you not like to try all sorts of lives – one is so very small – but that is the satisfaction of writing – one can impersonate so many people.

* * *

Care no more for the opinions of others, for those voices. Do the hardest thing on earth for you. Act for yourself. Face the truth.

* * *

I have such a horror of telegrams that ask me how I am! I always want to reply dead.

* * *

It's a terrible thing to be alone – yes, it is, it is – but don't lower your mask until you have another mask prepared beneath – as terrible as you like – but a mask.

* * *

The truth is that every true admirer of the novels cherishes the happy thought that he alone – reading between the lines – has become the secret friend of their author.

* * *

MARGARET SANGER

Margaret Sanger (born Margaret Louise Higgins, September 14, 1879 – September 6, 1966) was an American birth control activist, sex educator, writer, and nurse. Sanger popularized the term "birth control," opened the first birth control clinic in the United States, and established organizations that evolved into the Planned Parenthood Federation of America. Sanger used her writings and speeches primarily to promote her way of thinking. She was prosecuted for her book Family Limitation under the Comstock Act in 1914. She was afraid of what would happen, so she fled to Britain until she knew it was safe to return to the US. Sanger's efforts contributed to several judicial cases that helped legalize contraception in the United States. Due to her connection with Planned Parenthood, Sanger is a frequent target of criticism by opponents of abortion. However, Sanger drew a sharp distinction between birth control and abortion and was opposed to abortion through the bulk of her career. Sanger remains an admired figure in the American reproductive rights movement. She has been criticized for supporting eugenics.

In 1916, Sanger opened the first birth control clinic in the United States, which led to her arrest for distributing information on contraception, after an undercover policewoman bought a copy of her pamphlet on family planning. Her subsequent trial and appeal generated controversy. Sanger felt that in order for women to have an equal footing in society and to lead healthier lives, they needed to be able to determine when to bear children. She also wanted to prevent so-called back-alley abortions, which were common at the time because abortions were illegal in the United States. She believed that while abortion was sometimes justified, it should generally be avoided, and she considered contraception the only practical way to avoid them.

In 1921, Sanger founded the American Birth Control League, which later became the Planned Parenthood Federation of America. In New York City, she organized the first birth control clinic staffed by all-female doctors, as well as a clinic in Harlem with an all African-American advisory council, where African-American staff was later added. In 1929, she formed the National Committee on Federal Legislation for Birth Control, which served as the focal point of her lobbying efforts to legalize contraception in the United States. From 1952 to 1959, Sanger served as president of the International Planned Parenthood Federation. She died in 1966 and is widely regarded as a founder of the modern birth control movement. [

* * *

But in my view, I believe that there should be no more babies.

* * *

The most merciful thing that the large family does to one of its infant members is to kill it.

* * *

We don't want the word to go out that we want to exterminate the Negro population...

* * *

I accepted an invitation to talk to the women's branch of the Ku Klux Klan... I was escorted to the platform, was introduced, and began to speak...In the end, through simple illustrations, I believed I had accomplished my purpose. A dozen invitations to speak to similar groups were proffered.

* * *

I think the greatest sin in the world is bringing children into the world, that have disease from their parents, that have no chance in the world to be a human being practically... Delinquents, prisoners, all sorts of things just marked when they're born. That to me is the greatest sin—that people can—can commit.

* * *

The most serious evil of our times is that of encouraging the bringing into the world of large families. The most immoral practice of the day is breeding too many children...

* * *

As an advocate of birth control, I wish to take advantage of the present opportunity to point out that the unbalance between the birth rate of the 'unfit' and the 'fit,' admittedly the greatest present menace to civilization, can never be rectified by the inauguration of a cradle competition between these two classes.

* * *

The most urgent problem today is how to limit and discourage the over-fertility of the mentally and physically defective.

* * *

No more children should be born when the parents, though healthy themselves, find that their children are physically or mentally defective.

* * *

A marriage license shall in itself give husband and wife only the right to a common household and not the right to parenthood.

* * *

Apply a stern and rigid policy of sterilization and segregation to that grade of population whose progeny is tainted, or whose inheritance is such that objectionable traits may be transmitted to offspring.

* * *

No woman shall have the legal right to bear a child,
and no man shall have the right to become a father,
without a permit for parenthood.
Permits for parenthood shall be issued upon
application by city, county, or state authorities to
married couples, providing they are financially able to
support the expected child, have the qualifications
needed for proper rearing of the child, have no
transmissible diseases, and, on the woman's part, no
medical indication that maternity is likely to result in
death or permanent injury to health.
No permit for parenthood shall be valid for more than
one birth...

* * *

Organized charity itself is the symptom of malignant
social disease...

* * *

My own position is that the Catholic doctrine is
illogical, not in accord with science, and definitely
against social welfare and race improvement.

* * *

Feeble-mindedness perpetuates itself from the ranks
of those who are blandly indifferent to their racial

responsibilities. And it is largely this type of humanity we are now drawing upon to populate our world for the generations to come. In this orgy of multiplying and replenishing the earth, this type is pari passu multiplying and perpetuating those direst evils in which we must, if civilization is to survive, extirpate by the very roots.

* * *

Birth control itself often denounced as a violation of natural law, is nothing more or less than the facilitation of the process of weeding out the unfit, of preventing the birth of defectives or of those who will become defectives... If we are to make racial progress, this development of womanhood must precede motherhood in every individual woman.

MARLENE DIETRICH

Maria Magdalena Dietrich (27 December 1901 – 6 May 1992)- German and American actress, singer, sex symbol. During her lifetime she became a legend, having created in the cinema one of the perfect female images and having a great influence on fashion, style and female consciousness.

* * *

It's the friends you can call up at 4 a.m. that matter.

* * *

Femininity: Woman's greatest asset. Her own magnetic field into which the man is drawn.

* * *

Arrogance: On some people, it looks good.

* * *

Forgiveness: Once a woman has forgiven her man, she must not reheat his sins for breakfast.

* * *

Harmony: I need harmony around me more than food, drink, and sleep.

* * *

Quotations: I love them because it is a joy to find thoughts one might have, beautifully expressed with much authority by someone recognizably wiser than yourself.

* * *

Manners: Good manners – know your place. Bad manners – meddle.

* * *

White bread: I cringe every time I see a child eating a sandwich made out of American white bread. Give them whole wheat or rye if you love them.

* * *

Cavalier: A species that is dying out.

* * *

Jeans: Sometimes I like entire towns or places just because I don't ever have to get out of my jeans.

* * *

Vices: What other people have. I dress for the image. Not for myself, not for the public, not for fashion, not for men.

* * *

Optimism: Have it. There is always time to cry later.

* * *

Sex: In America an obsession. In other parts of the world a fact.

* * *

Habit: Often mistaken for love.

* * *

Mother: More solid than the ground under your feet when you are little, more solid than rock when you need to lean, harder than rock when the learning becomes a danger – when it's time for you to walk alone.

* * *

Tolerance: Teach it to your children. It is most important to the saving of their souls.

* * *

Stupidity: The only defect with which I can lose my patience.

* * *

Most women set out to try to change a man, and when they have changed him, they do not like him.

* * *

Peace: Why does it elude us so frequently, when it is so sincerely desired?

* * *

A country without bordellos is like a house without bathrooms.

* * *

Gossip: Nobody will tell you gossip if you don't listen.

* * *

Unmade bed: A man would rather come home to an unmade bed and a happy woman than to a neatly made bed and an angry woman.

* * *

Sex is much better with a woman, but then one can't live with a woman.

* * *

Kisses: Don't waste them. But don't count them.

* * *

Patience: Patience can become second nature if taught early enough. One of those gifts to your children for which you will be hated first and loved later.

* * *

Negligence: Unforgivable.

* * *

Jealousy: An uncontrollable passion, the Siamese twin of love.

* * *

Glamour is what I sell, it's my stock in trade.

* * *

Xmas: An abbreviation which should be forbidden by the police.

* * *

Tact: Some people have a natural built-in tact of the heart. If you know one, treat him gently; they are hard to come by. But tact can be taught; best when we are young, and not by words but by example.

* * *

Grumbling is the death of love.

* * *

In Europe, it doesn't matter if you're a man or a woman – we make love with anyone we find attractive.

MARILYN MONROE

Marilyn Monroe (1926–1962) was an American actress, comedienne, singer, and model. She became one of the world's most enduring iconic figures and is remembered both for her winsome embodiment of the Hollywood sex symbol and her tragic personal and professional struggles within the film industry. Her life and death are still the subjects of much controversy ...

* * *

Imperfection is beauty, madness is genius, and it's better to be absolutely ridiculous than absolutely boring.

* * *

I am good, but not an angel. I do sin, but I am not the devil. I am just a small girl in a big world trying to find someone to love.

* * *

I believe that everything happens for a reason. People change so that you can learn to let go, things go wrong so that you appreciate them when they're right, you believe lies, so you eventually learn to trust no one but yourself, and sometimes good things fall apart so better things can fall together.

* * *

I'm selfish, impatient and a little insecure. I make mistakes, I am out of control and at times hard to handle. But if you can't handle me at my worst, then you sure as hell don't deserve me at my best.

* * *

Success makes so many people hate you. I wish it weren't that way. It would be wonderful to enjoy success without seeing envy in the eyes of those around you.

* * *

If you can make a girl laugh, you can make her do anything.

* * *

A wise girl kisses but doesn't love, listens but doesn't believe, and leaves before she is left.

* * *

It's better to be unhappy alone than unhappy with someone.

* * *

We should all start to live before we get too old. Fear is stupid. So are regrets.

* * *

It's often just enough to be with someone. I don't need to touch them. Not even talk. A feeling passes between you both. You're not alone.

* * *

I don't know who invented high heels, but all women owe him a lot.

* * *

Keep smiling, because life is a beautiful thing and there's so much to smile about.

* * *

You never know what life is like until you have lived it.

* * *

A career is wonderful, but you can't curl up with it on a cold night.

* * *

I live to succeed, not to please you or anyone else.

MICHELLE OBAMA

Michelle LaVaughn Robinson Obama (born January 17, 1964, is an American lawyer, university administrator, and writer who served as the First Lady of the United States from 2009 to 2017. She is married to the 44th U.S. President, Barack Obama, and was the first African-American First Lady. Raised on the South Side of Chicago, Illinois, Obama is a graduate of Princeton University and Harvard Law School. In her early legal career, she worked at the law firm Sidley Austin, where she met Barack Obama. She subsequently worked in non-profits and as the Associate Dean of Student Services at the University of Chicago and the Vice President for Community and External Affairs of the University of Chicago Medical Center. Michelle married Barack in 1992, and they have two daughters.

As First Lady, Obama served as a role model for women and worked as an advocate for poverty awareness, education, nutrition, physical activity, and healthy eating. She supported American designers and was considered a fashion icon.

With the ascent of her husband as a prominent national politician, Obama became a part of popular culture. In May 2006, Essence listed her among "25 of the World's Most Inspiring Women. In July 2007, Vanity Fair listed her among "10 of the World's Best Dressed People." She was an honorary guest at Oprah Winfrey's Legends Ball as a "young'un" paying tribute to the "Legends" who helped pave the way for African-American women. In September 2007, magazines listed her 58th of 'The Harvard 100'; a list of the prior year's most influential Harvard alumni. Her husband was ranked fourth. In

July 2008, she made a repeat appearance on the Vanity Fair international best-dressed list. She also appeared on the 2008 People list of best-dressed women and was praised by the magazine for her "classic and confident" look.

Obama has been compared to Jacqueline Kennedy due to her sense of style, and also to Barbara Bush for her discipline and decorum. Obama's style has been described as "fashion populist." In 2010, she wore clothes, many high ends, from more than 50 design companies with less expensive pieces from J. Crew and Target, and the same year a study found that her patronage was worth an average of $14 million to a company. She became a fashion trendsetter, in particular favoring sleeveless dresses, including her first-term official portrait in a dress by Michael Kors, and her ball gowns designed by Jason Wu for both inaugurals. She has also been known for wearing clothes by African designers such as Mimi Plange, Duro Olowu, Maki Oh, and Osei Duro, and styles such as the Adire fabric.

* * *

The difference between a broken community and a thriving one is the presence of a woman who is valued.

* * *

Walk away from friendships that make you feel small and insecure, and seek out people who inspire you and support you.

* * *

Real men treat the janitor with the same respect as the CEO.

* * *

When someone is cruel or acts like a bully, you don't stoop to their level. No, our motto is, when they go low, we go high.

* * *

Success is only meaningful and enjoyable if it feels like your own.

* * *

Instead of letting your hardships and failures discourage or exhaust you, let them inspire you. Let them make you even hungrier to succeed.

* * *

You're important in your own right.

* * *

Whether you come from a council estate or a country estate, your success will be determined by your own confidence and fortitude. No country can ever truly flourish if it stifles the potential of its women and deprives itself of the contributions of half of its citizens.

* * *

Success isn't about how much money you make, it's about the difference you make in people's lives.

* * *

When girls are educated, their countries become stronger and more prosperous.

* * *

Choose people who lift you up.

* * *

Don't be afraid. Be focused. Be determined. Be hopeful. Be empowered.

* * *

How hard you work matters more than how much you make.

* * *

Failure is an important part of your growth and developing resilience. Don't be afraid to fail.

* * *

Just do what works for you because there will always be someone who thinks differently.

* * *

Being president doesn't change who you are – it reveals who you are.

* * *

You may not always have a comfortable life, and you will not always be able to solve all of the world's problems at once but don't ever underestimate the importance you can have because history has shown us that courage can be contagious and hope can take on a life of its own.

* * *

We need to start focusing on what matters – on how we feel, and how we feel about ourselves.

* * *

Every girl, no matter where she lives, deserves the opportunity to develop the promise inside of her.

* * *

Just try new things. Don't be afraid. Step out of your comfort zones and soar.

* * *

I am an example of what is possible when girls from the very beginning of their lives are loved and nurtured by people around them. I was surrounded by extraordinary women in my life who taught me about quiet strength and dignity.

* * *

Every day, you have the power to choose.

* * *

Empower yourselves with a good education.

* * *

Do not bring people in your life who weigh you down, and trust your instincts. Good relationships feel good. They feel right. They don't hurt. They're not painful. That's not just with somebody you want to marry, but it's with the friends you choose. It's with the people you surround yourself with.

* * *

The one way to get me to work my hardest was to doubt me.

* * *

There is no magic to achievement. It's really about hard work, choices, and persistence.

* * *

You should never view your challenges as a disadvantage. Instead, it's important for you to understand that your experience facing and overcoming adversity is actually one of your biggest advantages.

* * *

I have learned that as long as I hold fast to my beliefs and values – and follow my own moral compass – then the only expectations I need to live up to are my own.

* * *

Don't ever make decisions based on fear. Make decisions based on hope and possibility. Make decisions based on what should happen, not what shouldn't.

* * *

Through my education, I didn't just develop skills, I didn't just develop the ability to learn, but I developed confidence.

* * *

There is no limit to what we can accomplish.

* * *

Failing is a crucial part of success. Every time you fail and get back up. You practice perseverance, which is the key to life. Your strength comes in your ability to recover.

* * *

The only limit to the height of your achievements is the reach of your dreams and your willingness to work hard for them

* * *

One of the lessons that I grew up with was to always stay true to yourself and never let what somebody says distract you from your goals.

NANCY ASTOR

Nancy Witcher Langhorne Astor (19 May 1879 – 2 May 1964), Viscountess Astor was the first female Member of Parliament to take her seat.

She was an American citizen who moved to England at age 26. She made a second marriage to Waldorf Astor as a young woman in England. After he succeeded to the peerage and entered the House of Lords, she entered politics, in 1919 winning his former seat in Plymouth and becoming the first woman to sit as a Member of Parliament (MP) in the House of Commons. [Note 1] Her first husband was an American citizen, Robert Gould Shaw II, and they divorced. She served in Parliament as a member of the Conservative Party for Plymouth Sutton until 1945, when she was persuaded to step down.

Nancy Shaw had already become known in English society as an interesting and witty American, at a time when numerous wealthy young American women had married into the aristocracy. Her tendency to be saucy in conversation, yet religiously devout and almost prudish in behavior, confused many of the English men but pleased some of the older socialites. Nancy also began to show her skill at winning over critics. She was once asked by an English woman, "Have you come to get our husbands?" Her unexpected response, "If you knew the trouble, I had getting rid of mine...." charmed her listeners and displayed the wit for which she became known

* * *

I married beneath me, all women do.

* * *

If I were your wife, I'd put poison in your coffee. If I were your husband, I'd drink it.

* * *

We, women, talk too much, but even then, we don't tell half what we know.

* * *

I used to dread getting older because I thought I would not be able to do all the things I wanted to do, but now that I am older, I find that I don't want to do them.

* * *

One reason I don't drink is that I want to know when I am having a good time.

* * *

A fool without fear is sometimes wiser than an angel with fear.

* * *

The trouble with most people is that they think with their hopes or fears or wishes rather than with their minds.

* * *

In passing, also, I would like to say that the first time Adam had a chance, he laid the blame on a woman.

* * *

The most practical thing in the world is common sense and common humanity.

* * *

Pioneers may be picturesque figures, but they are often rather lonely ones.

* * *

The main dangers in this life are the people who want to change everything or nothing.

* * *

Dreams are great. When they disappear, you may still be here, but you will have ceased to live.

* * *

Women have got to make the world safe for men since men have made it so darned unsafe for women.

* * *

Truth always originates in a minority of one, and every custom begins as a broken precedent.

* * *

Take a close-up of a woman past sixty? You might as well use a picture of a relief map of Ireland!

* * *

My vigor, vitality, and cheek repel me – I am the kind of woman I would run from.

* * *

Real education should educate us out of self into something far finer; into a selflessness which links us with all humanity.

* * *

The only thing I like about rich people is their money.

OPRAH WINFREY

Oprah Winfrey is often praised for overcoming adversity to become a benefactor to others. From 2006 to 2008, her endorsement of Barack Obama, by one estimate, delivered over a million votes in the close 2008 Democratic primary race and led to Obama winning the election. In 2013, she was awarded the Presidential Medal of Freedom by President Obama and honorary doctorate degrees from Duke and Harvard. Oprah Winfrey (born January 29, 1954) is an American media executive, actress, talk show host, television producer, and philanthropist. She is best known for her talk show The Oprah Winfrey Show, which was the highest-rated television program of its kind in history and was nationally syndicated from 1986 to 2011 in Chicago. Dubbed the "Queen of All Media," she was the richest African American of the 20th century and North America's first black multi-billionaire and has been ranked the greatest black philanthropist in American history. She has also been sometimes ranked as the most influential woman in the world.

Winfrey was born into poverty in rural Mississippi to a teenage single mother and later raised in an inner-city Milwaukee neighborhood. She has stated that she was molested during her childhood and early teens and became pregnant at 14; her son died in infancy. Sent to live with the man she calls her father, Vernon Winfrey, a barber in Tennessee, she landed a job in radio while still in high school and began co-anchoring the local evening news at the age of 19. Her emotional ad-lib delivery eventually got her transferred to the daytime talk show arena, and after boosting a third-rated local Chicago talk show to first place, she launched her own production company and became internationally syndicated.

By the mid-1990s, she had reinvented her show with a focus on literature, self-improvement, and spirituality. Though criticized for unleashing confession culture, promoting controversial self-help ideas, and having an overly emotion-centered approach,

* * *

Don't worry about being successful but work toward being significant and the success will naturally follow.

* * *

Surround yourself only with people who are going to take you higher.

* * *

You can have it all. Just not all at once.

* * *

Turn your wounds into wisdom.

* * *

Where there is no struggle, there is no strength.

* * *

Do the one thing you think you cannot do. Fail at it. Try again. Do better the second time. The only people who never tumble are those who never mount the high wire. This is your moment. Own it.

* * *

We can't become what we need to be by remaining what we are.

* * *

As you become more clear about who you really are, you'll be better able to decide what is best for you – the first time around.

* * *

The more you praise and celebrate your life, the more there is in life to celebrate.

* * *

Listen to the rhythm of your own calling, and follow that.

* * *

Be thankful for what you have; you'll end up having more. If you concentrate on what you don't have, you will never have enough

* * *

The greatest discovery of all time is that a person can change their future by merely changing their attitude.

* * *

You become what you believe.

* * *

I don't think of myself as a poor deprived ghetto girl who made good. I think of myself as somebody who, from an early age, knew I was responsible for myself, and I had to make good.

* * *

Use your life to serve the world, and you will find that also serves you.

* * *

Failure is a great teacher. If you're open to it, every mistake has a lesson to offer.

* * *

What I know is that if you do work that you love, and the work fulfills you, the rest will come.

* * *

You can have it all. Just not at once.

* * *

Luck is a matter of preparation meeting opportunity.

* * *

Go ahead, fall down. The world looks different from the ground.

* * *

All my life I have wanted to lead people an empathy space. To a gratitude space. I want us all to fulfill our greatest potential. To find our calling, and summon the courage to live it.

* * *

You know you are on the road to success if you would do your job, and not be paid for it.

* * *

Failing is another stepping stone to greatness.

* * *

Follow your instincts. That is where true wisdom
manifests itself.
You cannot hate other people without hating yourself.

* * *

The biggest adventure you can ever take is to live the
life of your dreams.

* * *

The big secret in life is there is no secret. Whatever
your goal. You can get there if you're willing to work.

* * *

Whatever you fear the most has no power, it is your
fear that has no power. Oprah Winfrey

* * *

Create the highest grandest vision for your life. Then
let every step move you in that direction.

* * *

The way through the challenge is to get still, and ask
yourself: What is the next right move?

* * *

The truth is I have from the very beginning listened to my instincts. All of my best decisions in life have come because I was attuned to what really felt like the next right move for me. Oprah Winfrey

* * *

I don't believe in failure. Failure is just information and an opportunity to change your course.

* * *

You get in life what you have the courage to ask for.

* * *

There is a flow with your name on it. Your job is to find it and let it carry you to the next level.

* * *

Doing the best at this moment puts you in the best place for the next moment.

* * *

The smallest change in perspective can transform a life. What tiny attitude adjustment might turn your world around.

* * *

The single greatest thing you can do to change your life today would be to start being grateful for what you have right now.

* * *

Trust that everything happens for a reason, even when you're not wise enough to see it.

* * *

Don't settle for a relationship that won't let you be yourself.

* * *

No experience is ever wasted. Everything has meaning.

* * *

The choice to be excellent begins with aligning your thoughts and words with the intention to require more from yourself.

* * *

Often, we don't even realize who we're meant to be because we're so busy trying to live out someone else's ideas. But other people and their opinions hold no power in defining our destiny.

* * *

Passion is energy. Feel the power that comes from focusing on what excites you.

* * *

With every experience, you alone are painting your own canvas, thought by thought, choice by choice.

* * *

I believe that one of life's greatest risks is never daring to risk.

* * *

What material success does is provide you with the ability to concentrate on other things that really matter. And that is being able to make a difference, not only in your own life but in other people's lives.

* * *

I know for sure that what we dwell on is who we become.

* * *

I had no idea that being your authentic self could make me as rich as I've become. If I had, I'd have done it a lot earlier.

* * *

Every time you state what you want or believe, you're the first to hear it. It's a message to both you and others about what you think is possible. Don't put a ceiling on yourself.

* * *

Your true passion should feel like breathing; it's that natural.

* * *

You have to know what sparks the light in you so that you, in your own way, can illuminate the world.

PRINCESS DIANA

Diana, Princess of Wales (1 July 1961 – 31 August 1997) was a member of the British royal family. She was the first wife of Charles, Prince of Wales, the heir apparent to the British throne, and the mother of Prince William, Duke of Cambridge, and Prince Harry, Duke of Sussex.

As Princess of Wales, Diana undertook royal duties on behalf of the Queen and represented her at functions overseas. She was celebrated for her charity work and for her support of the International Campaign to Ban Landmines. Diana was involved with dozens of charities including London's Great Ormond Street Hospital for children, of which she was president from 1989. She also raised awareness and advocated ways to help people affected with HIV/AIDS, cancer, and mental illness.

Diana remained the object of worldwide media scrutiny during and after her marriage, which ended in divorce on 28 August 1996 following well-publicized extramarital affairs by both parties. Media attention and public mourning were extensive after her death in a car crash in a Paris tunnel on 31 August 1997 and subsequent televised funeral.

* * *

Everyone needs to be valued. Everyone has the potential to give something back.

* * *

Carry out a random act of kindness, with no expectation of reward, safe in the knowledge that one day someone might do the same for you.

* * *

I wear my heart on my sleeve.

* * *

A family is the most important thing in the world.

* * *

Only do what your heart tells you.

* * *

Every one of us needs to show how much we care for each other and, in the process, care for ourselves.

* * *

Life is just a journey.

* * *

They say it is better to be poor and happy than rich and miserable, but how about a compromise like moderately rich and just moody?

* * *

Hugs can do great amounts of good – especially for children.

* * *

If you find someone you love in your life, then hang on to that love.

* * *

The greatest problem in the world today is intolerance. Everyone is so intolerant of each other.

* * *

When you are happy, you can forgive a great deal.

* * *

I don't want expensive gifts; I don't want to be bought. I have everything I want. I just want someone to be there for me, to make me feel safe and secure.

* * *

I touch people. I think everyone needs that. Placing a hand on a friend's face means making contact.

* * *

Helping people in need is a good and essential part of my life, a kind of destiny.

* * *

I'd like to be a queen in people's hearts

* * *

Anywhere I see suffering, that is where I want to be, doing what I can.

* * *

I don't go by the rulebook; I lead from the heart, not the head.

* * *

You can't comfort the afflicted with afflicting the comfortable.

* * *

I think the biggest disease the world suffers from in this day and age is the disease of people feeling unloved. I know that I can give love for a minute, for half an hour, for a day, for a month, but I can give. I am very happy to do that, I want to do that.

SALLY KRISTEN RIDE

Sally Kristen Ride (May 26, 1951 – July 23, 2012) was an American astronaut, physicist, and engineer. Born in Los Angeles, she joined NASA in 1978 and became the first American woman in space in 1983. Ride was the third woman in space overall, after USSR cosmonauts Valentina Tereshkova (1963) and Svetlana Savitskaya (1982). Ride remains the youngest American astronaut to have traveled to space, having done so at the age of 32. After flying twice on the Orbiter Challenger, she left NASA in 1987. She worked for two years at Stanford University's Center for International Security and Arms Control, then at the University of California, San Diego as a professor of physics, primarily researching nonlinear optics and Thomson scattering. She served on the committees that investigated the Challenger and Columbia space shuttle disasters, the only person to participate in both. Ride died of pancreatic cancer on July 23, 2012

* * *

The stars don't look bigger, but they do look brighter.

* * *

When you're getting ready to launch into space, you're sitting on a big explosion just waiting to happen.

* * *

I've discovered that half the people would love to go into space and there's no need to explain it to them. The other half can't understand, and I couldn't explain it to them. If someone doesn't know why I can't explain it.

* * *

All adventures—especially into new territory—are scary.

* * *

I think there probably is life, maybe primitive life, in outer space. There might be very primitive life in our solar system — single-cell animals, that sort of thing.

* * *

The stars don't look bigger, but they do look brighter.

* * *

Studying whether there's life on Mars or studying how the universe began, there's something magical about pushing back the frontiers of knowledge.

* * *

I suggest taking the high road and have a little sense of humor and let things roll off your back.

* * *

Suppose you came across a woman lying on the street with an elephant sitting on her chest. You notice she is short of breath. Shortness of breath can be a symptom of heart problems. In her case, the much more likely cause is the elephant on her chest. For a long time, society put obstacles in the way of women who wanted to enter the sciences. That is the elephant.

* * *

If we want scientists and engineers in the future, we should be cultivating the girls as much as the boys.

* * *

The view of earth is absolutely spectacular, and the feeling of looking back and seeing your planet as a planet is just an amazing feeling. It's a totally different perspective, and it makes you appreciate, actually, how fragile our existence is.

* * *

I have been a bit of a risk taker all my life.

* * *

If I think I've accomplished what I set out to accomplish, then that's an achievement.

* * *

Try to understand who you are and what you want to do, and don't be afraid to go down that road and do whatever it takes and work as hard as you have to work to achieve that.

* * *

It's also critical to prepare the core of the future skilled workforce. That's because in the next decade or so, fully 80 of the jobs in this country, that includes basic living wage jobs, are going to require some background in science, math or technology.

* * *

I never went into physics or the astronaut corps to become a role model. But after my first flight, it became clear to me that I was one.

* * *

I'm not a goal-oriented person. I don't look out into the future and say, 'Five or ten years from now, this is what I want to be doing, this is where I want to be.' I'm very much a person who gets very, very involved in whatever I happen to be doing now.

SOPHIE KINSELLA

Madeleine Sophie Wickham also knew under the pen name Sophie Kinsella (born 12 December 1969) is an English author of chick lit. The first two novels in her best-selling Shopaholic series, The Secret Dreamworld of a Shopaholic and Shopaholic Abroad, were adapted into the film Confessions of a Shopaholic (2009). Her books have been translated into over 30 languages.

At the age of 24, while working as a financial journalist, Wickham wrote her first novel. The Tennis Party was immediately hailed as a success by critics and the public alike and became a top ten best-seller. She went on to publish six more novels as Madeleine Wickham: A Desirable Residence, Swimming Pool Sunday, The Gatecrasher, The Wedding Girl, Cocktails for Three and Sleeping Arrangements.

Kinsella is best known for writing the Shopaholic novels series of chick lit novels, which focus on the misadventures of Becky Bloomwood, a financial journalist who cannot manage her own finances. She is also known for her relationship with Luke. The series focuses on her obsession with shopping and its resulting complications for her life. The first two Shopaholic books were adapted into a film and released in February 2009. [citation needed.

The most recent addition to the Shopaholic series, "Shopaholic to the Rescue" was released on 22 October 2015. Her most recent standalone novels are My Not So Perfect Life and Surprise Me. In 2015, she branched into Young Adult writing with her first YA book, Finding Audrey, published in

June 2015.

A musical adaptation of Kinsella's novel 'Sleeping Arrangements' by Chris Burgess was premiered on 17 April 2013 in London at the Landor Theatre

* * *

There's no luck in business. There's an only drive, determination, and more drive.

* * *

Darling, when things go wrong in life, you lift your chin, put on a ravishing smile, mix yourself a little cocktail...

* * *

I love new clothes. If everyone could just wear new clothes every day, I reckon depression wouldn't exist anymore.

* * *

Sometimes you don't need a goal in life, you don't need to know the big picture.
You just need to know what you're going to do next!

* * *

No human on God's earth is a nobody.

* * *

If you can't be honest with your friends and colleagues and loved ones, then what is life all about?

* * *

Life would be a lot easier if conversations were rewindable and erasable, like videos. Or if you could instruct people to disregard what you just said, like in a courtroom.

* * *

Still, that's the point of love – you love someone despite their flaws.

* * *

Some things are best left a blur. Births and Visa bills.

* * *

A man will never love you or treat you as well as a store. If a man doesn't fit, you can't exchange him seven days later for a gorgeous cashmere sweater. And the store always smells good. A store can awaken a lust for things you never even knew you needed. And when your fingers first grasp those shiny new bags...

* * *

Never give up on something you really want. However impossible things seem, there's always a way.

* * *

The thing with giving up is you never know. You never know whether you could have done the job. And I'm sick of not knowing about my life.

* * *

Everyone knows revenge is a dish best served when you've had enough time to build up enough vitriol and fury.

* * *

I'm Cinderella. No, I'm better than Cinderella, because she only got the prince, didn't she? I'm Cinderella with fab teeth and a shit-hot job.

* * *

People who want to make a million borrow a million first.

* * *

The truth is, some relationships are supposed to last forever, and some are only supposed to last a few days. That's the way life is.

SOPHIA LOREN

Sofia Villani Scicolone, known by her stage name Sophia Loren (born 20 September 1934) is an Italian film actress and singer. Encouraged to enroll in acting lessons after entering a beauty pageant, Loren began her film career in 1950 at age 16. She appeared in several bit parts and minor roles in the early part of the decade until her five-picture contract with Paramount in 1956 launched her international career. Notable film appearances around this time include The Pride and the Passion, Houseboat, and It Started in Naples.

Her talents as an actress were not recognized until her performance as Cesira in Vittorio De Sica's Two Women; Loren's performance earned her the Academy Award for Best Actress in 1962 and made her the first actress to win an Oscar for a foreign-language performance. She holds the record for having earned six David di Donatello Awards for Best Actress: Two Women; Yesterday, Today and Tomorrow; Marriage Italian Style (for which she was nominated for a second Oscar); Sunflower; The Voyage; and A Special Day. After starting a family in the early 1970s, Loren chose to make only occasional film appearances. In later years, she has appeared in American films such as Grumpier Old Men (1995) and Nine (2009).

Aside from the Academy Awards, she won a Grammy Award, five special Golden Globes, a BAFTA Award, a Laurel Award, the Volpi Cup for Best Actress at the Venice Film Festival, the Best Actress Award at the Cannes Film Festival, and the

Honorary Academy Award in 1991. In 1995, she received the Golden Globe Cecil B. DeMille Award for lifetime achievements, one of many such awards. In 1999, Loren was acknowledged as No. 21 of the top 25 female American screen legends in the American Film Institute's survey, AFI's 100 Years...100 Stars, and she is currently the only living actress on the list.

* * *

Nothing makes a woman more beautiful than the belief that she is beautiful.

* * *

Everything you see I owe to pasta.

* * *

Sex is like washing your face – just something you do because you have to. Sex without love is absolutely ridiculous. Sex follows love, it never precedes it.

* * *

There is a fountain of youth: It is your mind, your talents, the creativity you bring to your life and the lives of people you love. When you learn to tap this source, you will have truly defeated age.

* * *

If you haven't cried, your eyes cannot be beautiful.

* * *

Many people think they want things, but they don't really have the strength, the discipline. They are weak. I believe that you get what you want if you want it badly enough.

* * *

When you are a mother, you are never really alone in your thoughts. A mother always has to think twice, once for herself and once for her child

* * *

The only people who never make mistakes are the ones who don't do anything. Mistakes are part of the dues one pays for living a full life.

* * *

It's a mistake to think that once you're done with school, you need never learn anything new.

* * *

If you can learn to use your mind as well as your powder puff, you will become more truly beautiful.

* * *

I've never tried to block out the memories of the past, even though some are painful. I don't understand people who hide from their past. Everything you live through helps to make you the person you are now.

* * *

Beauty is how you feel inside, and it reflects in your eyes. It is not something physical.

* * *

I hated my father all my life, but in his final days, I forgave him for all the suffering he caused us. As you grow older, marry, and have children of your own, you learn and forget. I do not forget easily, but I do forgive.

* * *

I was not interested in what I could bring to myself by being an actress, but in what I could bring out of myself.

* * *

I'm not Italian, I am Neapolitan! It's another thing.

* * *

It is very important for an actor or actress to look around at everything and everyone and never forget about real life.

* * *

True happiness is impossible without solitude.... I need solitude in my life as I need food and drink and the laughter of little children. Extravagant though it may sound, solitude is the filter of my soul. It nourishes me and rejuvenates me. Left alone, I discovered that I keep myself good company.

* * *

When – Sophia Loren is naked, that is a lot of nakedness

* * *

Being beautiful can never hurt, but you have to have more. You have to sparkle, you have to be fun, you have to make your brain work if you have one.

* * *

The facts of life are that a child who has seen war cannot be compared with a child who doesn't know what war is except from television.

* * *

You give but little when you give of your possessions. It is when you give of yourself that you truly give.

* * *

I think the quality of sexiness comes from within. It is something that is in you, or it isn't, and it really doesn't have much to do with breasts or thighs or the pout of your lips.

* * *

My philosophy is that it's better to explore life and make mistakes than to play it safe and not to explore at all.

* * *

Sex appeal is fifty percent what you've got and fifty percent what people think you've got.

* * *

I do not have a set regimen of exercise. The only activity I really enjoy is swimming. And I love to walk for long distances.

* * *

I firmly believe we can make our own miracles if we believe strongly enough in ourselves and our mission on earth.

* * *

I always wake up early and jump out of bed – sometimes not wanting to, because one can always find an alibi not to exercise – and then I take a walk for an hour. And as I walk around the park I always think, maybe around the corner, I am going to find something beautiful. I always think positively. It is very rare that you find me in a mood that is sad or melancholic.

* * *

The two big advantages I had at birth were to have been born wise and have been born in poverty.

* * *

A woman's dress should be like a barbed-wire fence, serving its purpose without obstructing the view.

YOKO ONO

Yoko Ono (born February 18, 1933) is a Japanese multimedia artist, singer, songwriter, and peace activist who is also known for her work in performance art and filmmaking. She performs in both English and Japanese. She is known for having been the second wife of singer-songwriter John Lennon of the Beatles.

Ono grew up in Tokyo and also spent several years in New York City. She studied at Gakushuin University, but withdrew from her course after two years and moved to New York in 1953 to live with her family. She spent some time at Sarah Lawrence College and then became involved in New York City's downtown artists scene, which included the Fluxus group. She first met Lennon in 1966 at her own art exhibition in London, and they became a couple in 1968 and wed the following year. With their performance Bed-Ins for Peace in Amsterdam and Montreal in 1969, Ono and Lennon famously used their honeymoon at the Hilton Amsterdam as a stage for public protests against the Vietnam War. The feminist themes of her music have influenced musicians as diverse as the B-52s and Meredith Monk. She achieved commercial and critical acclaim in 1980 with the chart-topping album Double Fantasy, a collaboration with Lennon that was released three weeks before his murder.

As Lennon's widow, Ono works to preserve his legacy. She funded Strawberry Fields in Manhattan's Central Park, the Imagine Peace Tower in Iceland, and the John Lennon Museum in Saitama, Japan (which closed in 2010). She has made significant philanthropic contributions to the arts, peace,

Philippine and Japan disaster relief, and other causes. In 2012 Ono received the Dr. Rainer Hildebrandt Human Rights Award. The award is given annually in recognition of extraordinary, nonviolent commitment to human rights. Ono continued her social activism when she inaugurated a biennial $50,000 LennonOno Grant for Peace in 2002. She also co-founded the group Artists Against Fracking in 2012. She has a daughter, Kyoko Chan Cox, from her marriage to Anthony Cox and a son, Sean Taro Ono Lennon, from her marriage to Lennon. She collaborates musically with Sean.

* * *

Everybody's an artist. Everybody's God.
It's just that they're inhibited.

* * *

When you go to war, both sides lose totally.

* * *

What the Beatles did was something incredible, it was more than what a band could do. We have to give them respect.

* * *

The sixties were about releasing ourselves from conventional society and freeing ourselves.

* * *

John wrote with a very deep love for the human race and a concern for its future.

* * *

Healing yourself is connected with healing to others.

* * *

I think one of the reasons that I'm surviving is the incredible negative power that was trying to erase me. It was not the truth that I broke up the Beatles.

* * *

I think of John every day. I do try to block it, but December 8th is not the only day I think of him.

* * *

I feel sad that he's just a voice now.

* * *

Remember, our hearts are one. Even when we are at war with each other, our hearts are always beating in unison.

* * *

Is truth always positive? Of course. Once the truth comes out, you know, it's all right. We're scared that if the truth comes out that it's not all right. It's the other way around.

* * *

A dream you dream alone is only a dream. A dream you dream together is a reality.

* * *

Marriage is a gamble, let's be honest.

* * *

In a day, sometimes I feel so much love for the world, I think my heart is bursting. Sometimes, I feel so scared, I want to shrink myself even further. I think that's what happened to us gods and goddesses. Like the dinosaurs, we realized that it's too dangerous to be so large. So we kept shrinking ourselves to what we are now. We might get even smaller. I see the sign in the engineers making smaller gadgets, smaller and smaller. Pretty soon, our fingers will be too large to operate them. So, what are we doing? I trust in human wisdom. We are incredibly intelligent beings. So, we might know something without thinking that we know... Well, even my best friend didn't know until now that I was thinking of crazy things like this.

* * *

Remember, each one of us has the power
to change the world.

* * *

I have a big job in addition to music:
to keep his voice going.

* * *

Spring passes, and one remembers one's innocence.
Summer passes and one remembers one's exuberance.
Autumn passes and one remembers one's reverence.
Winter passes, and one remembers one's perseverance.

* * *

Each time we don't say what we want to say, we're
dying.

* * *

True artists are prophets. I don't want to be that
prophetic in that sense because it's so lonely.

* * *

I saw that nothing was permanent. You don't want to
possess anything that is dear because you might lose it.

* * *

I don't know if I've learned so much from people as from events. Events are the best teacher for us. You try to learn from people, there is always some bend to it.

* * *

It's better to dance than to march through life.

* * *

I thought art was a verb, rather than a noun.

* * *

At least I had that, one guy understood me.

* * *

I didn't think I would be a widow. Nobody thinks they are going to be a widow. And the minute I was a widow, I started to see what a test it is to be a widow in this society.

* * *

The opposite of love is fear, not hate.

* * *

MORE QUOTES

We must develop a thick skin. With an unshakeable sense of self – and a commitment to being compassionate – nothing will faze you. (Mari Smith, Social Media Marketer known as the Facebook Queen).

* * *

Nasty Gal would have surely failed had it been my goal to grow a business to the size that I have today. (Sophia Amoruso, Nasty Gal founder and author of Girl Boss).

* * *

Do the best you can in every task, no matter how unimportant it may seem at the time. No one learns more about a problem than the person at the bottom. (Sandra Day O'Connor, the first woman appointed to the Supreme Court).

* * *

I want little girls to grow up knowing they can do anything, even play football. (Jen Welter, the NFL's first female coach).

* * *

Champions keep playing until they get it right. (Billie Jean King, American tennis player who fought for equal prize money for female athletes).

* * *

I hope you will find some way to break the rules and make a little trouble out there. And I also hope that you will choose to make some of that trouble on behalf of women. (Nora Ephron, screenwriter).

* * *

To love what you do and feel like it matters, how could anything be more fun? (Katherine Graham, first American female Fortune 500 CEO).

* * *

Everybody gets so much information all day long that they lose their common sense. (Gertrude Stein, American author).

* * *

When I'm hungry, I eat. When I'm thirsty, I drink. When I feel like saying something, I say it. (Madonna, American entertainer and first female billionaire of pop music).

* * *

Ask for what you want and be prepared to get it. (Maya Angelou, author of Why the Caged Bird Sings, the first nonfiction best-seller by an African-American woman).

* * *

I attribute my success to this: I never gave or took any excuse. (Florence Nightingale, nurse).

* * *

Decide...whether or not the goal is worth the risks involved. If it is, stop worrying. (Amelia Earhart, pilot).

* * *

Our theory is, if you need the user to tell you what you're selling, then you don't know what you're selling, and it's probably not going to be a good experience. (Marissa Mayer, CEO of Yahoo, the youngest CEO of a Fortune 500 company).

* * *

If you follow your heart, if you listen to your gut, and if you extend your hand to help another, not for any agenda, but for the sake of humanity, you are going to find the truth. (Erin Brockovich, environmental activist).

* * *

The secret of staying young is to live honestly, eat slowly, and lie about your age. (Lucille Ball, the first woman to head a major Hollywood television studio).

* * *

I was taught to strive not because there were any guarantees of success but because the act of striving is in itself the only way to keep faith with life. (Madeleine Albright, first female U.S. Secretary of State).

* * *

Every great dream begins with a dreamer. (Harriet Tubman, African-American abolitionist).

* * *

Be less curious about people and more curious about ideas. (Marie Curie, first female Nobel Prize recipient).

* * *

There are lots of opportunities out there for women to work in these fields, girls just need support, encouragement and mentoring to follow through with the sciences. (Sally Ride, first American female to go into space).

* * *

Some leaders are born women. (Geraldine Ferraro, first female Vice-Presidential candidate).

* * *

To stay ahead, you must have your next idea waiting in the wings. (Rosabeth Moss Kanter, academic and business leader who coined terms such as empowerment and employee participation).

* * *

Each person must live their life as a model for others. (Rosa Parks, civil rights activist).

* * *

There are no ugly women, only lazy ones. (Helena Rubenstein, American businesswoman who started one of the world's first cosmetic companies).

* * *

Do not be afraid to make decisions. Do not be afraid to make mistakes. (Carly Fiorina, first female CEO of a Fortune 20 company).

* * *

I always want to make films. I think of it as a great opportunity to comment on the world in which we live.

(Kathryn Bigelow, the first female to win an Academy Award for Best Director).

* * *

I was probably, definitely, not normal. I was reading Moby Dick from start to finish when I was about nine. I read a ton of books. I still have a notebook with a complete design for a time machine that I designed when I must have been, like, seven. The wonderful thing about the way I was raised is that no one ever told me that I couldn't do those things. - Elizabeth Holmes, founder of Theranos and America's youngest female billionaire).

* * *

The price of inaction is far greater than the cost of a mistake. (Meg Whitman, the first female to run two large U.S. public companies, eBay and HP).

* * *

If we are going to be part of the solution, we have to engage the problems. (Majora Carter, urban revitalization strategist).

* * *

You create opportunities by performing, not complaining. (Muriel Siebert, first female member of the New York Stock Exchange).

* * *

None of us can know what we are capable of until we are tested. (Elizabeth Blackwell, the first woman to graduate from medical school in the U.S.)

* * *

If you obey all of the rules, you miss all of the fun. (Katherine Hepburn, actress).

* * *

Women and cats will do as they please, and men and dogs should relax and get used to the idea. (Robert A. Heinlein).

* * *

I never dreamed about success. I worked for it. (Estee Lauder).

* * *

Define success on your own terms, achieve it by your own rules, and build a life you're proud to live. (Anne Sweeny).

* * *

I didn't know what I wanted to do, but I always knew the woman I wanted to be. (Diane Von Furstenberg).

* * *

I always believed that one woman's success can only help another woman's success. (Gloria Vanderbilt).

* * *

Delete the negative; accentuate the positive. (Donna Karan).

* * *

I always did something I was a little not ready to do. I think that's how you grow. When there's that moment of 'wow I'm not really sure I can do this,' and you push through those moments, that's when you have a breakthrough. (Marissa Mayer).

* * *

A confident woman, a woman who truly knows her worth and her power is a force to be reckoned with. (Mandy Hale).

* * *

Success isn't about how much money you make, it's about the difference you make in people's lives. (Michelle Obama).

* * *

The most courageous act is still to think for yourself. Aloud. (Coco Chanel).

* * *

I alone cannot change the world, but I can cast a stone across the waters to create many ripples. (Mother Teresa).

* * *

Honor your calling. Everyone has one. Trust your heart, and success will come to you. (Oprah Winfrey).

* * *

It's never too late to make a comeback. (Christina Katz).

* * *

Only do what your heart tells you. (Princess Diana).

* * *

If this is something that you really want to do if you believe in it...simply keep forging forward because success will come. (Cassandra Sanford).

* * *

I think the key is for women not to set any limits. (Martina Navratilova).

* * *

Always remember that you are absolutely unique. Just like everyone else. (Margaret Mead).

* * *

You may encounter many defeats, but you must not be defeated. (Maya Angelou).

* * *

Faith is the strength by which a shattered world shall emerge into the light. (Helen Keller).

* * *

Trust your gut. (Sara Blakely)

* * *

When you're building a business, you're either all in, or you're not. (Barbara Corcoran).

* * *

Don't waste a single second. Just move forward as fast as you can, and go for it. (Rebecca Woodcock).

* * *

As you grow older, you will discover that you have two hands, one for helping yourself, the other for helping others. (Audrey Hepburn).

* * *

If your actions create a legacy that inspires others to dream more, learn more, do more and become more, then, you are an excellent leader. (Dolly Parton).

* * *

You have to do what you dream of doing, even while you're afraid. (Arianna Huffington).

* * *

Happiness is the gradual realization of a worthy ideal or goal. (Florence Nightingale).

* * *

Really take the time to focus on finding your voice and making sure that whatever you're creating is of high

quality and is useful for people in their everyday lives.
(Brit Morin).

* * *

If it doesn't scare you, you're probably not dreaming
big enough. (Tory Burch).

* * *

You get what you give. What you put into things is
what you get out of them. (Jenifer Lopez)

* * *

Anything is possible if you've got enough nerve. (JK
Rowling)

* * *

Be the kind of woman that makes other women want to
be you. Topaz
I am not afraid...I was born to do this. (Joan Of Arc).

* * *

Women are as capable as men, and this needs to be the
focus of our education, that women can be whatever
they want to be.
(DJ Sinhala).

Made in the USA
Monee, IL
19 January 2023

25691914R00138